The Art of Essential Action

Learn how you can use time, action, and space to see your vision effectively so you can build wealth at a faster pace…

A Financial Guide for Taking "Essential Action" and Using "Time Management" More Wisely so that You Can Build Wealth Efficiently in Any Economy

TFA Financial Planning books are available at special quantity discounts for those who desire to purchase in large quantities. For more information please email: tj@thewealthincreaser.com.

Thomas (TJ) Underwood

Library of Congress Cataloging-in-Publication Data

ISBN: *978-1-953994-27-1*

Publisher: TFA Financial Planning

Printed in the United States of America

Self-Published

Text design by Thomas (TJ) Underwood

Contents

Foreword

It is important that you realize that you can utilize the time that you have available while you are here on planet earth more advantageously as you build wealth. At the current stage in your life, it is important that you and others who desire lasting success learn how to use the "power of time" to achieve more financially throughout your lifetime.

Isn't the time right for you to learn how you can more effectively manage your time and learn other wealth building concepts that you can implement in your life that can propel you and your family forward and help you reach your goals in the 21st century and beyond.

In this one-of-a-kind book, **The Art of Essential Action,** which was created for those who need to be kicked in the rear for them to shift into the right gear (metaphorically speaking), so that real results that move them towards their goals in a meaningful manner and be achieved efficiently, is now near.

If procrastination is a part of your personal profile, you must know in certain terms that you can reverse the process and create an active personality where you can consistently get things done in a timelier manner, and **The Art of Essential Action** is a book that can help direct you toward what you need to do, to better ensure that what you desire most has a real chance of coming true.

In the current economy many are having detrimental thoughts that are acting as a drag on the progress that they are and can make, and **The Art of Essential Action** can help you and others who need to attain major goals, do just that in a timelier manner so that you can make your life more meaningful on a daily basis.

If you are one who on occasion “say to yourself” that you are:

Good for Nothing

I’m good for nothing on this day!

Nothing is going my way!

I know that I need to do more!

But the steps that I take leave me even more unsure!

I’m currently facing adversity from all angles!

And I know that I need to pursue goals that I can untangle!

On this day I’m good for nothing, however I am committed to turning my current situation into something!

I am committed to giving it my best and I am determined to reach a higher level of success!

The Art of Essential Action is designed to put you on a more successful path toward managing your financial affairs and help you build wealth in a timelier manner in any economic environment.

Introduction

It is important that you never give up, you must look onward and upward in your credit, financial, and all areas of your life so that you can see your future with more clarity!

It is important that you act in a timely manner on all matters of importance in your life, and specifically as you build wealth. You must always realize that you can change your future into one of true success if you continue to have faith, you put together a serious plan for future success and you gain the right knowledge along with a clear understanding of how to execute and apply that knowledge in your everyday life in the most efficient manner possible!

In many cases your future success could be imminent or years away! The key is that you must never give up! I have seen many past clients who stayed focus and pressed on despite the adversity that they faced and by doing so they were able to attain the success (goals) that they desire to achieve most.

In many cases they were able to succeed beyond their own expectations because they stayed focused and followed an effective plan of action as best they could, considering their circumstances!

The point is, if you stop believing and aspiring to reach your goals or let the adversity that you will undoubtedly face affect you in the wrong way—you may become a loser (you may not reach the goals and objectives that you desire)!

However, if you press on and always believe that better days lie ahead and you take the right action on a daily basis to work toward making those better days occur in a real and serious manner, major success can happen in your life!

On the other hand, if you stop believing that true success is in your future and you don't take the right steps that are necessary to work towards success, you will more than likely fall short of success. As you take action to improve upon the happenings in your life, there are a few "must do's" that you want to do to further ensure that your dreams will come true.

Must Do's:

You must believe—if you want to achieve!

You must know—before true success will show!

You must let your mind mentally ascend—or it will descend!

You must defeat your fears—and always realize that miracles can sometimes take years!

Onward and upward—your mind must go—otherwise your success level will be low!

In order to get a definite level of satisfaction, you must have a written plan of action!

You must put together a plan that will give you the clear "vision" to make your future goal(s) and objective(s) a reality. You must dream big and put together a plan that is powerful and will motivate you at a very high level.

You must have a system in place that allows you to not only formulate a vision, but you must have a system that gives you the working knowledge that is needed to attain that vision.

Starting today, you can make future success go your way.

Reading **"The Art of Essential Action"** now—will show you how!

Just as I did not expect others to put into action the vision that I had for the creation of this book, you must not expect others to put into action the vision that you have about your future, whether it be improving your credit, finances or any other goal or dream that you may have!

Even though I was hopeful that others would provide a book that addressed credit and finance issues of concern of consumers around the world in a comprehensive manner that would truly benefit them in a really beneficial way, that did not occur!

Therefore, I took action (dreamed big) and brought this book into existence to attain that objective, and you can do the same if you have a powerful vision that can truly be of benefit to yourself, your family and others!

In short, only you can see what you see and only you can put into action what you see and make it a reality for the world to see!

Be sure to use your "mental vision" to attain the goals that you desire for yourself and your family, and never give up as excuses and falling short of big dreams are for those who are **not fully committed to their vision**—not YOU!

You must realize that by having a powerful vision and every intention on reaching that vision, you will "distinguish yourself from the crowd" once you bring into existence that vision.

You must always realize that if you don't want success—success does not want you!

You must also realize that if you are consistently around others who dream big, you will also begin to dream big! On the flip side if you are constantly around losers—you too will be a loser unless you develop dominant thoughts (many of which are presented in this book) that are positive and moves you in the right direction in spite of being around losers!

It is also important that you realize that everything that comes to you as a vision may not be the vision that is for you or the vision that you should act on! You must be able to discern if you have a clear vision and also discern whether that clear vision is the one that you should act on.

If your vision is truly worth acting on you will see it clearly and you won't complain, worry, feel inadequate, lack initiative, want others to do it in your absence, or have a pessimistic view of your future!

Quite the contrary—you will accept the vision and you will see major success (your energy level will increase and you will take direct action) and your path to that success will be clear in your mind because the only outcome that is possible is the success that you see!

You must see your future clearly (have a clear vision of your future)—always love, honor, and believe in yourself and always know that the success that you desire lies in the horizon if you continue to press on and take the necessary action on a consistent basis!

*Did you know that by **V**iewing your future with **I**nspiration you can **S**ee your future clearly and bring out what is **I**nside **O**f you—something that is truly **N**ew?*

Along the way you must never let the adversity that you will undoubtedly face change your dream or vision, because you have true vision. You must press on in a determined manner regardless of the adversity that you will face along the way!

By pressing on in a determined manner, you are putting yourself on a major path toward success—starting today!

In **"The Art of Essential Action"** you will learn the importance of acting timely on a consistent basis so that you can achieve more throughout your lifetime, and particularly as you build wealth.

All the best toward unlimited success, in large part because "you" decided to "enhance your view of your future" and give it your absolute best...

A Word About Taking Effective Action and Effectively Building Wealth

A **new and more empowering way of thinking** and **taking action** as it relates to **accumulating wealth** can be yours if you make the decision to prepare your mind for the journey and you are willing to expend the needed effort and time to make it all happen.

You can change your life significantly by utilizing your mind to ask the right questions and seek the right answers—at the right time!

Isn't it time you dare to dream big, take bold action, act with confidence (never feel that you are too old or too young, out of shape, mentally unequipped, lacking the time, money, talent, skills or education) and change your thoughts and your future for the better?

Did you know that you often won't get what you want in life, but **you will get what you prepare for** at the various stages of your life cycle?

Isn't the time right on your calendar to **prepare your mind for success today** by making a commitment to attain a **Financially Alert Mind**—this year?

Did you know that **lack of preparation** is the "key to failure" for those who don't succeed in reaching their goals and objectives?

It is important that you **schedule your future success** to happen with more certainty by **visualizing your future** **and** **utilizing written goal setting.** You must plan, take action and make real change happen over time—birth in your mind today what you desire to happen in your future, and then pursue what you really desire with a higher level of enthusiasm so that you can make it happen in real time!

A **financially alert mind** is proactive and addresses credit and financial concerns on the front end, and will put you in better control of your financial future.

A **financially alert mind** knows how to properly utilize personal financial statements, properly manage and improve personal credit and properly address all areas of personal finance that needs to be addressed.

A **financially alert mind** does so in an effective and efficient manner and in a manner that benefits those who have a financially alert mind the most—not creditors and others who have no real concern for their or their family's livelihood!

Your dreams can happen! It is important that you never lose your fire on the inside, and you must vigorously pursue what is already yours—once you have **prepared your mind** properly!

Keep in mind that reaching your goals and obtaining a **financially alert mind** will take discipline! You must have a mature mindset and you must choose between what you want **now**—or what you want **most.**

Choosing what you want most demonstrates maturity and signals you are ready to manage your finances wisely and achieve your major goals.

What is stopping you from moving forward and finding the inspiration to come up with your own solutions to many of the questions that you now have about your personal finances? Be sure to utilize this book so that you can utilize your abilities in a more **financially alert manner** and achieve more while you are here on earth.

Did you know that when your mind is ready to receive—the answer will be presented to you? A **financially alert mind** will help put your mind in position to receive what serves your best interest because you will then have the **preparation** and **knowledge** of what it takes to build and maintain a **solid credit and finance foundation** at the **various stages in your life.**

It is important that you are conscious of what goes into your mind and heart daily. **The Art of Essential Action** answers many of the questions that you may have if you are willing to make a sincere effort to comprehensively address your personal finances in a more **financially alert manner** so that you can achieve what you truly desire as you journey forward.

Financially Alert Mind versus Financial Literacy

Since the real estate and financial market downturn in 2008, many financial advisors and money watchers have approached personal finance with a new attitude. Many more now see the need to educate consumers to make them more **financially literate** in a proactive manner—as they realized that once hardship is encountered, it often takes years to rectify. The goal of financial literacy is to help consumers avoid the mishaps that were often made during that volatile period that began in 2007 and continued for several years thereafter.

It is important that you realize that **financial literacy** is a good starting point but will not really take you to **where you truly need to be,** if you are one who sincerely wants to manage your credit and finances in a more effective and efficient manner and achieve lasting results.

It is uplifting to see that more financial advisers and planners are now looking more at "behavioral finance" or the "psychological aspects" of financial moves that consumers make—because that behavior and thinking has a huge effect on how consumers manage their money throughout their lifetime, regardless of their money management personality or economic environment in which they operate in.

As one of a small number of financial planners who have looked deeply into the **behavior of consumers for decades,** I have long realized that what consumers lack is a **comprehensive approach** to managing their credit and finances that they can "carry within" their mind and heart, easily understand—

and apply at the various stages in their life—with the potential for confusion **minimized or eliminated** as a key feature.

In a nutshell, **successful money management** often comes down to having the right approach!

Many approaches in the financial industry that are currently on the market are too complex or are not readily understood (lacks clarity for the average mind) by consumers in a clear and cohesive manner!

Over the years I have learned in depth that **"money management personalities"** can help or hinder consumers in the management of any financial management system, and particularly those systems and approaches that are difficult to understand and apply in a practical manner.

It is important that those who are in the financial industry, especially if you are a financial adviser or financial planner, have a real understanding of the **mental aspects of financial planning,** because successful financial planning consists of more than just understanding demographics, numbers, and creating personal financial statements.

The real key in the current economy or any economy includes having a real understanding of the role that **habits and personality types** play with today's consumers and money managers.

There can be a big difference between a **highly informed money manager personality** type and a **struggling money manager personality** type.

For financial advisors or financial planners, it is important to know **the differences among personality types, what their clients really value and other mental factors** that once were ignored by planners—but should no longer be ignored due to the importance that the factors have on the long-term success of consumers. In short, you as a financial planner must probe deeper and really determine the goals that your client values. If you are doing your own financial planning, you must do so with a spirit of excellence to be the most effective, and you too will have to probe deeper to determine where you really want to go (know in certain terms the goals that you desire to achieve).

If you are pursuing the management of your finances and you want to do so at a higher level, you must be aware of "how" you manage your finances and you must then put together a "comprehensive plan" for improvement!

It is true that **financial literacy** needs to begin in grade school and continue throughout high school and college, however spending more time educating consumers about fundamental financial tools such as balancing their checkbook, thinking about their own income statement, determining what percentage of their income goes to savings, spending, bills, charity, etcetera—in of itself is somewhat outdated.

Many consumers had that knowledge prior to the real estate and financial market downturns that occurred in 2008—yet they failed to apply that knowledge and use their literacy skills in a manner that benefited them and their family the most.

Many fell prey to "unwise decision making" and made financial outlays that "did not serve their best interests" due in large part to the urging of so-called professionals (attorneys, realtors, loan officers' etcetera) and many ended up in an even deeper financial hole.

In the mortgage industry in particular, many consumers knew or had an inkling that they were purchasing too much house or obtaining the wrong loan, but they were caught up into what everyone else was doing and ignored what they were feeling—in large part based on the suggestions of those who did not have their best interests in mind.

Financial literacy provides you with the opportunity to pay more attention to financial affairs in your life and not get caught up in the hysteria or excitement of the moment to a degree, however **you should have the goal of attaining more than just financial literacy** if you desire lasting financial success.

If you sincerely desire to take control of your finances, your goal should be to obtain a **"financially alert mind"** as it will provide you not only the **financial literacy that you need**, but will also provide you a new way to utilize the financial knowledge that you will soon learn to your and your family's true benefit for the rest of your life.

Those who have a "**financially alert mind"** cannot be easily taken advantage of because they have a system that "they can carry within their mind" that allows them to address their pressing financial concerns in a proactive and highly effective way.

Those who have a **financially alert mind** know how to invest in a manner that serves their best long-term interests and they cannot be led astray by scammers and others who do not have their best interest in mind.

Part of showing your love to your family and yourself is having a **"Financially Alert Mind"**—meaning you must know how to respond appropriately to all that happens in your financial life.

*By being financially alert, you will be of the mindset that **you must act** in a **proactive manner** as you move toward improving your credit and finances!*

By having a "financially alert mind" you will make it a priority to gain the preparation and knowledge that are needed for success on the front end, not after you have encountered financial difficulty.

Why Having a Financially Alert Mind Is So Important?

A **Financially Alert Mind** allows you to do your own thinking, allows **you** to **"take action"** on your own initiative, and **empowers YOU** with the ability to achieve the goals that serve your and your family's best interest.

You won't have to be forced or inspired by others to act, you will act on your own initiative to create the future that you desire!

By gaining the knowledge that you need to succeed you put yourself in position to take your credit and financial success higher so that you can achieve the goals that you and your family desire.

By making a real commitment to use your mind in a **financially alert manner,** you can put yourself in position to achieve your and your family's financial mission!

By opening your mind up to what is possible you put yourself in control of your credit and finances and your ability to secure your future!

Obtaining a **financially alert mind** is about empowering you with the **mental working knowledge** that you need so that "you" can succeed!

Did you know that if you have the self-discipline, proper preparation, proper focus and the right knowledge that is necessary you can effectively manage many or all of the credit and financial affairs in your life?

Always realize that if you can control your thought process and direct your actions the right way, you can control your future!

You can choose to "build up" your future or "tear down" your future by your daily thoughts and by the actions that you take on a consistent basis!

Did you know that a **F**inancially **A**lert **M**ind **I**mproves **L**ives **Y**early?

By having a **Financially Alert Mind** you can put yourself and your family in position to reach many or all of the future goals that you desire and you can position yourself to attain the goals that can make a real difference in your and your family's life!

You can now show your **LOVE** to your family and benefit your **F A M I L Y** and yourself by having a **Financially Alert Mind**—this year!

As a result of purchasing **The Art of Essential Action**, major success lies in your and your family's future. You can now sincerely pursue a path that will help you attain a financially alert mind in an efficient and highly effective way, in large part because of your decision to take action today.

By having a "financially alert mind" you will make it a priority to gain the preparation and knowledge that is needed for success on the front end—not after you have encountered financial difficulty.

A "financially alert mind" is organized and quick to see opportunity and at the same time realizes that there are no limitations on what it can accomplish because those who have a financially alert mind—don't set any limitations within their own mind! Use the **Triple A** action of a "Financially Alert Mind" to always know:

A *financially alert mind is proactive and addresses credit and financial concerns on the front end!*

A *"financially alert mind"* knows how to properly utilize personal financial statements, properly manage and improve their credit and properly address all areas of their finances that need to be addressed!

A *financially alert mind* does so in an effective and efficient manner and in a manner that benefits those who have a financially alert mind the most—not creditors and others who have no real concern for their or their family's livelihood!

You must make it a priority to utilize your mind properly and to think for yourself on important financial matters if you sincerely desire success on a consistent basis!

A **financially alert mind**—allows you the opportunity to do just that!

It is important that you realize that **financial personalities affect financial planning,** often in a significant way. Some personality types are financially independent, they are comfortable taking risks and they are confident that their income will last throughout their lifetime because they have planned in a strong manner, therefore financial concerns can be addressed efficiently.

Still others may need to be held by the hand and get to a level of understanding where they really see the need for comprehensive planning and how implementing a comprehensive plan can help them achieve their goal(s) more effectively and more efficiently. Regardless of where you fall on the "money personality" spectrum**, The Art of Essential Action** is designed to guide you on a more effective and efficient path as far as the management of your finances are concerned.

As someone who desires to be a serious money manager, **you must get your mind to a point where you can address all areas of your finances in a manner** that puts you in control and keeps you in control. You no longer must accidentally improve your credit and finances. You no longer must accidentally hurt your credit and finances!

You can now manage and improve your credit and finances in an **intentional manner** by obtaining a **Financially Alert Mind** and not just **Financial Literacy,** starting today and continuing throughout your lifetime!

It is the goal of **The Art of Essential Action** to get your mind in position to act timelier on the important financial matters in your life so that you can live daily with more joy and do what you desire throughout the various stages of your life.

An authentic, bold, confident, and daring approach must be utilized by you if you desire to achieve more as you navigate life. The Intricacies of wealth building can be simplified if you have the right approach and a high level of determination, and you are sincerely ready to get the ball moving at this time. In a real effort to take you toward the success that is most beneficial to you, **The Art of Essential Action** has simplified wealth building concepts and approaches that are highly effective so that you can utilize them to make your dreams come true! It is very important that you build the foundation that you need so that you can truly succeed from this day forward.

All the best...

About the Author

Thomas (TJ) Underwood is the creator of **TheWealthIncreaser.com**, one of the leading financial blogs that can be found in the blogosphere and is a former fee-only financial planner, former top producing loan processor and is currently an active real estate broker at **Realty 1 Strategic Advisors**. He is also the first financial planner to coin the phrase **"Financially Alert Mind"** and he has been serving consumers in personal finance for over 20 years!

Thomas (TJ) Underwood is a **licensed real estate broker** in the State of Georgia. He is also the broker/owner of **Realty 1 Strategic Advisors, LLC** which he founded in 2002. A pioneer in the real estate industry, his company is one of only a handful of real estate companies in existence that offer clients comprehensive financial planning as a part of the home buying and home selling process as a complimentary service.

You will usually find him assisting home buyers, home sellers and those who are trying to improve their financial position in the Atlanta Metropolitan area and throughout the world—improve their finances in an **intelligent, consistent, and proactive manner** at the various stages of their life.

Chapter 1 Time Management & Action Basics

The time to start anything meaningful in your life will never be to your liking...

It is important that you realize that the **"time"** to start improving your credit and finances will never be **"just right"** in your life!

Many consumers delay or worse yet never get around to managing and improving their wealth building effectively, in large part due to procrastination.

If that type of behavior applies to you, it is important that you realize that **now is the time** that you make a serious commitment to take action in your credit, financial, and all areas of your life that needs addressing!

If you eliminate procrastination and other negative qualities in your life, you put yourself in position for a **more effective use** of your time.

When you cultivate positive habits of success you begin to defeat all of the following and other negative qualities in your life and you will then be in position to make better use of your time:

- Critical spirit—always criticizing others
- Jealousy—being envious of the accomplishments of others
- Greed—pursuing prosperity in the wrong manner
    - Unforgiveness—negatively affects your spirit
    - Deceit—you can't fool yourself or others
- Anger—negatively affects your spirit
- Slander—attacking others in the wrong manner
- Love of money—you can still make a lot of it but put it in proper perspective
- Distractions—tend to lead you in the wrong direction

- Idolatry—sports, money, women, men
- Bitterness—if you have a bitter spirit, you can't be loved
- Lust—desire out of control
- Boastful Pride—on many occasions it is often best that you be humble in your accomplishments

It is very important that you understand why you must have **positive qualities of success** operating inside of your mind and heart on a consistent basis. By cultivating "positive habits of success" to a high level you put yourself in position to use your **"time"** in a wise manner and in a manner where you can really use your "mental energy" and "mental focus" to reach **the goals that you and your family desire** or need to achieve!

It is your responsibility to identify, acknowledge, and **take responsibility** for what is holding you and your family back in your wealth building activity and cultivate positive habits of success to a high level in your life in a timely manner so that you can eliminate or reduce the effects that "any negative qualities" may have on your life!

Your **self-discipline** in regards to the effective use of your time will help determine your destiny! You must have the **mindset** that you will budget your **time** wisely and **never make excuses**, if you really want (or need) to achieve at a high level!

You **must not have an attitude** that operates on when I get to a certain point in my life I will "then" get serious about my financial future.

If you are waiting on the one day when things in your life will be just right before you seriously start on your financial journey to success, you are robbing yourself and your loved ones of the possibility of achieving much more during your lifetime.

The **proper and effective use of your time** is a major factor in helping you reach your and your family's goals and objectives in a more efficient manner.

Many inefficient or weak money managers set goals in their mind and never get around to accomplishing them **due to poor usage of their time** and an improper application of their faith and belief system.

They often fail to take action in a meaningful way in many areas of their life by failing to make a sacrifice!

You must always believe in yourself and know deep down in your heart and mind that you will be successful in accomplishing your **future goals** because you know deep within that you are willing to expend the time and effort that is necessary!

Many inefficient money managers live their life in a manner where they do not effectively manage their time and when they get older, they look back and wonder—**what could have been?**

Don't let that be you!

Make effective use of your time starting now so that you can "really" reach the goals that you and your family desire!

You can **more effectively utilize your time** by formulating a "vision" of that which you want to occur by using written goal setting as a guide and gaining the right knowledge (proper preparation) prior to (or while) on your financial planning journey.

In addition, by comprehending and applying what you will learn in this book, you can **save valuable time** if you are now ready to make a serious commitment toward the improvement of your and your family's credit and finance position and other areas of your life that may need to be addressed more effectively.

The time to do what you need to do financially to achieve your goals will vary depending on where you are now at in your life stage, your current financial position, your money management personality, and the specific goals that you desire to achieve.

In the current economy in many parts of the world many are at a point where they are forced to analyze their income and living arrangements at a deeper level due to turbulence and uncertainty in the economy.

Many are now using their time wisely and are **looking within** in an introspective manner to see what they can possibly do better in their life in all areas, and particularly as it relates to the management of their finances and the building of wealth.

It is important that you too, **at this time** determine where you are now at financially and otherwise, and make the best or most optimal moves "at this time" based on your current life stage, financial position and vision that you have of the success that you want to achieve and are determined to achieve in your future.

It is important that you learn how you can use your time more wisely and achieve at a higher level at this time, and in your future by doing the following:

Plan for uncertain times...

You can use your time more wisely by focusing and planning on what you desire to occur in your future. Many of those who have taken the right action over a number of years (consistency in action) are now in a better position than most to handle the uncertainty and anxiety that is in the atmosphere at this time and are well positioned for future turbulence in any economic environment.

Whether it be financial or otherwise, you make the likelihood of future success occurring in your life when you plan for success, and particularly when you put your planning in writing.

You can use personal financial statements to see where you are now at and use the information that is derived from those statements to see where you can not only go, but need to go.

You must plan for success by knowing how credit works and using that knowledge to manage your credit in a manner that serves your best interests, not creditors.

You must plan and take the right posture daily if you truly desire to position yourself and your family for lifelong success!

It is also important that you have a comprehensive overview of your finances so that you can plan daily in a manner where you can win consistently. Even if you now find yourself in an adverse position as a result of happenings in the current economy or other factors that are unique to you, you must always know that you can put "rebound mechanisms" in place and still achieve your goals throughout your lifetime.

Know what you desire in your future...

You also want to take the time right now, to do some **deep thinking** to determine where you really want to take your future.

What were you put on earth to do?

Use the time that you now have to search through your mind, heart, and soul to determine if what you are now doing or working toward achieving is what you were truly put on earth to do!

Or, is what you are doing at this time something that you must do, but it serves no real end toward making your dreams come true—nor is it your purpose for being while you are here on earth?

It is important to use a calming approach (you slow your mind down and receive the inspiration and dreams that were meant for you) and look within to see your future with more clarity and determine if there is a better, more effective way of achieving what you really desire.

-

Do continuous review to make your dreams come true...

Once you put your plans into action you must still have the mindset that you will do continuous review and fine tune when and where necessary.

You can achieve many of your goals that you may now feel are out of reach if you take the time now to plan, do, and review.

By doing so **consistently** you can achieve at a higher level and fatigue, adversity, and a feeling of doubt will play no meaningful role in preventing you from **achieving your dreams**.

You can at this time choose to get down on yourself and remain where you are now at, or move along in life at a snail's pace, or you can use **the time that you have** to look within and plan for a better and brighter future that you can realistically make happen during your lifetime.

You can better prepare yourself and your family for the perils that lie ahead (both seen and unseen) and position yourself to "weather any storm" in a way where you come out in a good position or possibly even in a better position than when you were experiencing the storm–or even a better position than you were in before the storm!

Your Need to Act at this Time...

As the seasons come and go, it is important that you take inventory at this time of how you operate daily as it relates to your finances. You want to know the future action that you plan on taking as soon as possible—or the lack of action that you may be inclined to take in an unplanned way, if you now lack motivation and are prone to procrastinate.

It is very important that you have a system that is doable by you and provides in clear terms what you need to do to travel on "a more certain path" toward making your dreams come true.

Your dream to be all that you can be, can be made clearer to you and can be a real possibility if you at this time have **the endurance** to do what you need to do!

Do you procrastinate, fail to plan and have no clue of what you need to do to make your dreams come true or do you approach your wealth building effort with confidence, clarity and a real action plan that will take you where you need or desire to be?

In the remainder of this chapter you will learn the importance of "moving to action" on a **consistent basis** so that you can win the majority of your races and avoid the financial catastrophes that other people who fail to run at the right pace–face!

You must be sincere in your desire to move forward financially...

If you often procrastinate or fail to take the needed action when it is time to do so, your inactivity could be robbing you and your family of **achieving much more** during your lifetime.

By failing to take action at this time you are letting the time value of money and compounding work against you as opposed to for you!

Therefore, you must have the determination at this time, or you must be fully committed to seek better ways of **reaching your goals that are of most significance to you,** so that you can build wealth more efficiently.

Your sincere wealth building approach and your willingness to cultivate the "keys to success" at a higher level could possibly get you out of your **"inactivity trap"** if you are one who often procrastinate.

By doing what is necessary in a timely manner, you can take your finances to a higher state and therefore ensure that your goals won't occur late.

You must have an effective plan of attack and know how you manage your finances...

With most who procrastinate or fail to take action in a timely manner, the reason for doing so is normally a lack of focus and a lack of understanding on a **"plan of attack"** that works with their mind and is designed to serve their best interest in the short, intermediate, and long-term.

By purchasing this book, you can now create a plan of attack that works with your mind and one in which you can implement with confidence! You can start the process by creating personal financial statements and mastering your credit at this time, not at a time in your future!

You can implement a plan for long-term success by analyzing and improving upon all areas of your finances including insurance, investments, taxes, education planning, estate planning/wills and retirement planning, thereby leading to a more relaxed and comfortable lifestyle for you and your family.

All the above steps that you need to take will be reiterated throughout this book so that your conscious and subconscious mind can absorb the material, and your comprehension and application of the steps can be implemented with more ease throughout your lifetime.

The **3 Step System** that you will learn throughout this book will be made even clearer in **Appendix B** and will put you in an even stronger position for a lifetime of success.

You can further enhance your financial knowledge in many areas by visiting **TheWealthIncreaser.com** and typing in your topic of concern in the search box.

You must not let adversity or unwanted occurrences deter or detour your effort toward success...

As well as you may implement the steps mentioned above along with other actions that you take, adversity and situations that you did not or cannot plan for will occur, as life happenings that you have not, or cannot plan for will almost invariably happen, even with the best of planning.

Therefore, it is *your responsibility* to continuously review, if you sincerely desire to make your dreams come true. You also want to **create an emergency fund** that is properly funded at the earliest point in **your life stage** so that you can mitigate the damage that adverse situations can create.

You must show a real desire to reach higher and achieve at or above the level that you desire. By doing so you will be in the know and you will **increase your cash flow** and achieve results that will show.

Even though on occasion we all need admonishing to stay on track, you want to get into a habit of acting on your own initiative, if you sincerely desire to reach your highest potential.

When working with financial planners or financial coaches, admonishment is often done from a position of getting those who need to **take action** (or take the right action) to do so in a more timelier manner in order for them to achieve their goals and live out their life with more meaning and with joy at the center.

Or another way of looking at it is, planners and coaches admonish their client(s) from a vantage point of "love" so that those who desire lasting wealth building success can achieve that success at a higher level of excellence and really do what they desire during "their" lifetime and even after they transition by effective estate planning.

If you are one who often procrastinate or fail to take action (or take the right action) on a consistent basis, you can change that now by **implementing the above steps** and your life can take a turn for the better.

You must never let **w**orry, **a**nxiety, **f**ear, **f**rustration, **l**ack of effort and **e**xcuses be a deterrent as you move about throughout your life as it relates to your finances from this point forward.

You no longer have to **w a f f l e** back and forth and wonder (or doubt) if the moves that you make will lead you on a real path to success as it relates to continuous positive movement in the management of your finances, if you make a **definitive choice** to move forward and give it your absolute best today!

By "eliminating or reducing inaction" in your life, you can **start (or continue more effectively) on a path to reaching your goals** and live out your life with more clarity where you can enjoy life in a manner and style that is more beneficial for you and your family.

Also, you want to realize that when it comes to improving your finances and building wealth more efficiently you can choose to **D**elay, **D**on't do it at all, or **D**o it now!

By choosing to "do it now"–you can truly gain the insight that is needed to manage your finances at a very high level and live your life more abundantly while here on earth.

By being **D**ecisive at this time and **D**etermined to **D**o what you need to do—you can put the right **3D** glasses on that can lead you toward the vision that you **d**eserve, the vision that is **d**esired by you, and the vision that is **d**oable by you–so that you can make your dreams come true.

It is important that you see your future with more clarity so that you can take the right action on a consistent basis to help you move toward your wealth building goals in a more sincere manner. By utilizing YOUR 3D glasses, **you can choose** to act and make the right moves during your lifetime!

- Delay

It is important that you have a "do it now" type of attitude as you cannot operate like 90% (author's unscientific estimate) of the population and put off what you could do now by stating to yourself that you will do it later.

In many cases that later is often too late or never comes, as many rob themselves of achieving meaningful goals because they "start too late" and are unable to reach their goals due to the clock running out—so to speak.

You have the opportunity to throw away the notion of delay and put procrastination at bay, so that you can get positive momentum rolling your way.

-

- <u>**Don't do it at all**</u>

Even worse than delay is the attitude of many who don't want to plan, have no desire to plan and they are (or seem to be) willing to take whatever life dishes out at them.

It is important that you realize that you have the ability to make favorable outcomes happen in your life if you prepare for the journey and you gain the right knowledge, you have confidence at the right level and you timely act.

Many around the world who once had the attitude (whether consciously or unconsciously) of letting their finances manage them, have **turned their situation around** and have achieved major success by changing their money management personality to that of a **winner**–and you can do the same.

-

- <u>**Do it now**</u>

Even if you now have the attitude of delaying what you need to do or not doing anything at all, you can change your habits and develop an attitude of "do it now" and **change the direction and trajectory of your life** in a way that you could possibly never imagine at this time.

Although the process of building wealth may appear daunting and difficult, the process is not as difficult as you think if you attack your finances in a highly effective and logical way!

It is in your best interest to leave worry, anxiety, fear, frustration, lack of effort and excuses behind and make a determined and highly focused effort on improving your financial position (and life) so that you can avoid financial strife.

You can choose to "**d**elay" and more than likely financial mishaps will come your way, you can choose to "**d**on't do it at all" and possibly fall or move along at a snail's pace or not at all–or you can choose to "**d**o it now" and you will soon learn how—as it relates to effective wealth building in this economic environment, or any economic environment.

Conclusion or Key Points

It is important that you actively pursue "a more direct path" to the success that you desire as you take steps to move higher and higher.

By choosing to be **active at this time** you are operating in a proactive manner and not like many who operate in a reactive manner!

You are showing a real concern for your finances and financial future and you should feel confident about actively managing your finances and pursuing your dreams at a higher level than most.

Even so, financial success (or any success) will not be given to you, it must be earned by you!

Part of reaching the success that you desire is knowing the action steps that you can (and need) take to make what you desire a reality in real time.

How long, how wide, and how high are your thought processes as it relates to your finances?

How deep and layered is your approach to wealth building?

How will you use the time that you have been granted here on earth to your and your family's benefit **whether financial** or **living in your purpose** at the **various stages** of your life?

Always realize that time is also a dimension, as we all have a limited amount of it and you must use the time that you have been granted on earth in a wise manner!

It is the desire of the author that this chapter has led to "a calming of your thoughts" and a "feeling of well-being within" about your future that cannot be shaken. Regardless of where you now stand, you must know that better days are ahead, and you can use what you have learned in this chapter as a base point to move forward and perform to "your" best advantage in all facets of your life!

In times of economic uncertainty, you must believe and know that you will come out on the other side in a stronger position for success, whether it be financial or otherwise!

You must also remember that the time to do what you need to do to make your dreams come true will never be ideal. You have purchased this book, and you can now get your future right, despite the disheartening news that you may hear on your radio or hear and/or see on your phone or TV tonight.

Those who are serious about their future have been utilizing "positive qualities of success" for years and they continue to enhance their mind and heart with those qualities, due in large part to the calming effect that it has on their daily mindset, financial life, and overall well-being.

For those of you who are new to the concept of enhancing areas in which you are weak in, continue to transform your future to that of true success once and for all, whether it be financial or otherwise by any means necessary, whether it be utilizing this book or other sources.

You must give it your very best as you work toward your success during these difficult times, and throughout your lifetime.

By **using your thought process in 3D** you will achieve results that **you can see** and move closer toward who you were meant to be.

You will embrace and be in pursuit of new ideas, theories, models and concepts as it relates to wealth building in a more engaging and rewarding way, from day to day.

When you broaden, deepen and shift your thought process in a focused manner as it relates to your financial condition and you challenge your mind to operate at a higher level of excellence, you are putting your mind in position to give it your absolute best and by doing so you can help direct your future outcomes and make the wealth building goals that you desire a reality.

3D thinking supports your thought movements in pursuit of new goals and expands your creative and imaginative thoughts!

Even though the topics in this chapter may be tough to think about and act on, you must know that it is something that you (and/or your financial planner) must do–even if the process seems boring–if you desire to retire and live out your life with dignity and purpose, and make your big dreams come true.

In short, by actively pursuing what you desire most, it will be your **d**iligence in searching out the best sources of financial advice, your **d**iscipline and willingness to learn and take **d**ecisive action when it is in your best interest to do so, along with focusing on what is truly important at the right time during your life that will lead to the accomplishments that you really desire.

All the best as you **actively** pursue **3-Dimensional** success as you build wealth **at this time** and throughout your lifetime.

Chapter 2 Procrastination & Wealth Building

Learn the importance of avoiding procrastination and setting deadlines for the achievement of your goals...

It is important that you take a **sincere look** at **how you manage your time** as it relates to your finances and all areas of your life. The effective use of your time is critical for your long-term wealth building success.

You want to know at the earliest time possible that procrastination is an enemy of you achieving success, in large part because by utilizing your time inappropriately you are not giving it your best!

It is also important that you realize that the **time aspect of wealth building** can be looked at from several different angles. In this chapter you will learn a few significant ways that **you can use time to build wealth more efficiently** in varying economic cycles.

You cannot **waste time** daily by not knowing where you stand financially, not understanding how credit affects your overall finances, and not having a comprehensive overview of how to manage your finances effectively in all areas!

It is important that you understand the importance of **time management** and further "direct your actions" toward ways that you can actually use the **management of your time** to **achieve more** throughout your lifetime in ways **you may have never imagined before,** but may need to be made a part of your makeup as you learn more and more.

By applying proven concepts, **many have managed their time effectively** and achieved more, and you can do the same. Also, those who **did not manage their time effectively**, in many cases fell short of reaching the goals that the desired or needed to achieve, and procrastination was often one of the major reasons.

By **managing your time** in as effective a manner as possible, you can put yourself and your family in position to achieve much more (including goals that you may now feel are **impossible** to attain) in a more efficient manner.

In the following paragraphs (more in-depth details are in Appendix B) **you will learn 3 highly effective ways** that will guide you in an effort to direct you toward your goals, and help you avoid procrastination so that you can make **better use of your time** and achieve more throughout your lifetime.

1) Manage Your Time Better by Knowing Your Current Financial Condition

If you are at this time serious about the management of your time as you build wealth you must know your current financial condition or your current financial strength (or weakness).

As stated in chapter 1 and reiterated here, you want to know the following in clear terms:

Do you have adequate income at this time that will allow you to achieve **your future goals** or do you need to get more income and/or cut expenses or do a combination of the two?

By **creating a budget or cash flow statement** you can put yourself in position to know what you can do on a monthly basis in "concrete terms" and know what amount of funds that you will have left (discretionary income) to pursue other areas of concern that you may have financially.

Even though **it will take time** to create and analyze a cash flow statement, **you will save far more time in the long run** because a budget or cash flow statement will help give you the direction that you can (or need to) go in a much clearer manner.

2) Manage Your Time Better by Managing Your Credit Optimally

Once you know where you stand financially from month-to-month, you must put together a plan to eliminate your debt and particularly your credit card debt (if you have any) to a manageable level or to a level where you are in control—and not keep your balance(s) at a level where creditors control you!

You must also learn how to **master the 5 credit factors** so that you can manage and control your credit throughout your lifetime.

Even though it may take **mental energy** and **time** to learn and effectively apply your mastery of the credit factors, you will put yourself in position to manage your credit throughout your lifetime in a manner that will get you real results in a time-efficient manner and in a manner that can put you on a track to attaining the goals that you desire or need to attain throughout your lifetime and even after you transition.

3) Manage Your Time Better by Having a Comprehensive Overview of Your Overall Finances

By knowing your current financial condition and having mastery over your credit, you are now ready to analyze and approach your finances from all angles!

You are ready to look at your insurance, investments, taxes, emergency fund, education planning, estate planning/wills and retirement planning in a more confident manner.

You are ready to **use your time effectively** because you know the importance of living your life in a manner where you don't leave doing what needs to be done, for others to do.

You are now seeing your future **more vividly** (comprehensively) and with **more focus** because you know that you can achieve the goals that you desire if you stick to the plan that you (or your financial planner) create based on the analysis of your unique financial position that **you (and/or your financial planner) spent the time** to analyze.

At this **time** you would know that **achieving financial freedom** is your mission and you have no intention on stopping until it is done, or you are in a much better financial position!

The **effective management of your time** may initially seem very difficult to you and that is not uncommon.

However, once you start applying what you have learned in this book on a consistent basis, your understanding and application of the process will be made easier and **you will eventually save much more time** in comparison to the effort that you expend upfront when you look back upon your life!

Even though financial mishaps and correcting mistakes due to carelessness and not knowing what might (or is happening) will occur during your life, they will be reduced, eliminated or made less relevant in your life because you will have an effective system that you carry within your mind throughout your life that allows you to achieve more in less time.

Even though you may have to exert more mental energy than you or your peers are accustomed to on the front end—you will ultimately get to a point where managing your finances and **your time** becomes second nature to you—if you are sincere in making your dreams come true.

You will become very efficient in managing your finances and you will achieve more **throughout your lifetime** and it will be due in large part to the **commitment that you made** at **this time** to **build your wealth** in a more engaging way—as far as exerting more mental energy on the front end—in a real effort to achieve or reach your goal(s) in a timelier manner!

Also, you want to know the **time frame** in which you will reach your goals—the answer to how long it will take will vary from person to person, and your objective(s) or where you want to go financially.

Your goals and objectives will differ from others as everyone has a unique financial position and goals that differ in all cases!

It is important that you let something original work its truth in your life. Equip your mind for lasting success, do good work that will lead you on a real path toward reaching your goals and use a comprehensive approach to manage your finances that will force you to make better use of your time on a consistent basis and achieve goals that are uniquely your own!

In this chapter you have learned that the time to start effectively managing your finances and leaving procrastination in the rear—is now. The process of achieving your goals will take time and the reaching of your ultimate goals will vary from person to person and family to family and the time factor will be unknown in many cases unless you put in place a **written plan** based on your unique financial position that will effectively guide you to your destination—if you are willing to follow that written plan in a sincere manner.

By doing so, you are equipping yourself for the continuous financial success that you desire and deserve in the current financial and political environment—or any environment—now or in your future.

Your knowledge alone of the material in this chapter is not enough, action toward reaching YOUR GOALS is what really counts at this time.

Those who truly desire success prepare for the consequences or outcomes that they desire in a proactive manner and have a secondary plan if the outcomes differ from what they desire. They always respond positively to adversity and have an action-oriented mindset!

Transforming your finances from where they are at this time, to where you need (or desire) them to be is normally a process (time is involved) and not an event (I can do it today and I am through) and it is imperative that you prepare your mind for the journey at this time with realistic timelines as the blueprint within your mind, and a written plan that will provide you the needed direction (outside of your mind)!

It is important that you move toward the goals that you set for yourself and your family in a timely and efficient manner. Did you know that desperation (when you are forced to do something) leads to you making quick and often bad decisions and choices?

As you move toward your financial goals you should not feel stressed out or frustrated about your finances. And a proactive approach to managing your finances will help significantly in controlling how you feel daily in a positive way.

It is important that you don't become **complacent** and comfortable where you are now at. The best time to gain the knowledge that you need is BEFORE you have to make a decision or choice, therefore it is imperative that you have a **proactive mindset** when it comes to managing your finances and now is the ideal time that you gain the preparation and knowledge that you need so that you can truly succeed.

How you perform **when things are not going your way** will determine if you are a winner! If you are inspired, dedicated and you decide to take the right action on a consistent basis, you can make positive change happen in your life.

Now is the time that you create and maintain success on a consistent basis and do what needs to be done on the front end!

Do you at this time desire to attain results that you can see?

You can now do so by reading **The Art of Essential Action,** so you can timely pursue who you were meant to be!

There must be congruence and agreement within your mind and heart on "what you think," "what you say" and "what you do" if you sincerely desire to make your wealth building dreams come true.

If something doesn't feel right in your finances or you feel your finances are out of balance, you can correct that by analyzing your current situation and coming up with a serious written plan that you believe in and you are committed to implementing in your life!

Learn How You Can Avoid Being Complacent by Responding Appropriately to Adversity When Managing Your Finances

In life, things (adversity) will occur that you never planned for, however you can overcome from the adversity that you will face (or that you are now facing) by **not being complacent** and taking an active role in ensuring that success will occur in your and your family's future.

Are you operating in balance? Do your thoughts, feelings, behavior and goals all line up with your values and beliefs and are you moving towards the goals that will serve your best interest in an efficient manner?

How you use your time, mind, heart, and manage your money demonstrates your sincerity and commitment to your goals!

Is your plan for managing your finances in sync with your thoughts and actions that you are taking at this time, along with your written goals?

If what you are hearing, seeing and doing is out of balance with where you truly want to go in your future you make the process of achieving your objectives much more difficult than it has to be, along with how difficult it should be!

Are you complacent in your daily activities?

Are you operating at a high level on a daily basis and truly working towards your goals with a **consistent plan of action** that will take you to where you need to be? Do you know how to go over, through or around roadblocks to success or avoid them altogether?

Learn Why You Must Have a Plan of Action While Managing Your Finances

By formulating a mental plan of action and then following up with a written plan, you can **improve your focus** and get started on a path to truly **reaching your goals** in all areas of your life.

You must get to a point where you will do what you plan on doing in an **intelligent, consistent and proactive manner** or another way of looking at it is, you must use your mind at your highest level and get to a point where you will do what needs to be done when it is the best time to do so!

When it matters most you must be in position to apply the knowledge and preparation that you have acquired to achieve the goals and outcomes that you desire in the most effective and efficient manner possible!

When you have a **consistent plan of action** that you utilize on a consistent basis, it may initially appear that you are going nowhere! However, you must know that you are eventually going somewhere! And if you plan in an **intelligent and proactive manner** you can reach your goals much more effectively and efficiently.

You can then move in the direction of your life purpose or what you were truly put on earth to do. By taking the right steps daily you can do something big for yourself, your family and society.

Today is the day that you make the decision or choice to take **decisive action** and not be **complacent or content** with where you are now at. Even if you feel you are very successful currently, the ability to do much more resides inside of you.

Now is the time that you do what you need to do as you make a serious effort toward making your dreams come true!

You want to have **B**alance, **E**nthusiasm and **D**esire daily so that you can truly reach higher levels and achieve beyond your dreams!

By having a plan of action, you put yourself in position to make more effective use of your time, therefore you put yourself in position to achieve your goals at a faster pace.

By having a sincere desire to cultivate a more active mindset, you put in motion the inner workings of your mind to work harder on your behalf, and help further ensure that what you desire to occur is more of a sure bet.

Your goal is not to turn back or toward unyielding ignorance that is now in the atmosphere, but to move forward so that you can truly grow.

You must realize that growth is often uncomfortable, as it should be as you are in essence reaching higher. Growth requires you to exert more effort so that you can grow stronger and empower you (with the right knowledge) so that you can do more in less time.

Furthermore; you want to know at the earliest point possible that procrastination should play no meaningful role in any area of your life.

All the best toward your timely wealth building success...

Chapter 3 Responsibility and Wealth Building

Learn Why "Taking Responsibility" for "Your Financial Future" is to be expected of YOU...

It is important that you take **"full responsibility"** for your credit and financial future.

You must realize that it is "you" who must put into motion a plan that will take you and your family to where you need or want to be!

Do you know that many suffer financially due to irresponsible credit and finance management, and not lack of income?

In this day and age, you can't depend on others to improve your credit and finances for you.

You must always have a winning attitude and have an optimistic view of your credit and financial future.

Your attitude toward how you feel about yourself and your financial future will play a large part in helping you reach the goals and objectives that you desire for yourself and your family.

It is Your Responsibility to Develop Habits of Success

You must have a high level of determination to really make the goals that you seek a reality. It is your responsibility to develop and cultivate positive habits of success if your goal is to move yourself and your family forward in a meaningful way! You must pursue sound physical health, have a positive mental attitude, have an energetic spirit, have the ability to control your thought process, have a big imagination (ability to dream big), and apply your faith daily, as all that falls under your purview and is your responsibility.

You must show loyalty to others if you want loyalty, plan your future with others to reach a common goal, appreciate your life now by acting daily, have a purpose for living, have a pleasing personality and take personal initiative on matters of significance in your life!

What You Must Always Do

You must always budget your time, always be intelligent in thought (think carefully, analytically, accurately and critically), always give or do more than is expected, always cooperate with others in an effective manner, always respond favorably to adversity, always have self-discipline and self-confidence at all times and always have an enthusiastic spirit—if you "really" want to succeed at a high level.

You must always have thoughts of success on a consistent basis as by doing so you will defeat negative thoughts and negative behavior that does not serve your or your family's long term interest.

Although you can never really accomplish the above fully—you must have the aspirations to do so at a level that is the best that is within you!

Your Mindset is Also Critical for Your Future Success

You must transform or renew your mind from the inside out and find new and more effective ways of thinking.

No one else can do it for you. It is your responsibility to formulate your mindset for a successful and prosperous future!

You have all that it takes on the inside to transform your mind and take your life in the direction that you desire.

From this day forward you must not look for others to do it for you and you must realize deep within that it is your responsibility to do so and you must make the commitment to do so at this time.

You can achieve great heights in your life if you have the desire too! You can cultivate habits of success to a high level and success will undoubtedly come if you have faith and "really" believe in your heart and mind that you can do it.

In this book you have much of what you need to transform your credit and finances in a major way and achieve major success!

However, it is your responsibility (totally within your "power" and "control") to bring a “high level” of determination, self-discipline, focus, personal initiative and other key action qualities of success to the table if you are "truly sincere" about improving your and your family’s credit and finances to a high level.

You are responsible for knowing about and understanding personal financial statements that can really benefit you and your family if used properly.

You are responsible for understanding how credit works and using that knowledge to manage and improve your and your family's credit and finance position from this day forward.

You are responsible for knowing that "written goal setting" is far superior to just thinking about your goals and then trying to reach your goals!

Always remember, that even though you may be paying for financial advice and/or the financial management of your funds—it is still "your responsibility" to understand your risks and do your "due diligence" when choosing a financial advisor or financial planner in as effective a manner as possible!
You are responsible for understanding your personal finances in a comprehensive manner and understanding the need for and "purpose" of a properly funded emergency fund that can provide added protection for you and your family.

It Is Your Responsibility to Act—Now

If you have the motivation on this day, positive credit and finance improvement is on the way!

You will set yourself apart, if you are now ready to start!

Real credit and finance solutions are now available to you on this day!

Will you make it a point to get started and put your plan into play?

You can no longer use "cost" or "difficulty of understanding" as an excuse!

Get started now and put this book to good use!

Success lives in you whether you believe it to be true!

As you move toward your financial goals you should not feel stressed out or frustrated about your finances and a proactive approach to managing your finances will help significantly in controlling how you feel on a daily basis.

It is important that you know (your responsibility) what is working in, for, through, around, and against you regarding your credit and finances?

Do you know what is working in, for, through, around and against you in your credit and finances?

Are creditor's benefiting off of your unwise use of credit or do you have a pay-off or pay-down plan in place that will take you to where you need to be?

Do you have an overall plan for success with your credit and finances (it is always best that you have an overall or comprehensive approach to your credit and finances) or are you looking at your credit and finances in isolation?

Why You Must Take Responsibility

By "taking responsibility" you will put your mind in position to overcome whatever you are facing!

If you are now facing a difficult time whether it be financial or otherwise, you may feel that you have a lot of reasons to quit.

However, you must realize that if you decide to press on and move forward in spite of the adversity that you are now facing or that you may face in your

future, you will be successful because you are already equipped (mental toughness) with what it takes to succeed.
However, if you don't believe that you are equipped (mental weakness)—you have already set yourself up for failure (you'll be a loser). You must never underestimate the power of your thoughts on a daily basis!

Likewise, if you see success in your future—no matter how difficult your life may be or whatever comes your way, you set yourself up for the future success that you see and deserve! Keep in mind that your journey may not be easy but you must know that you will get there!

What You Must Do Now

You must realize that by "taking responsibility" for your future you can achieve much more than you anticipate and much more than you may have previously expected.

If you prepare your mind for future success by obtaining the knowledge that is necessary and you apply that knowledge effectively in your everyday life, your responsible use of your mind will be rewarded with success beyond your imagination! At this point in time and space you must determine if you are a "do it now—direct action type of person" or are you one who will often procrastinate?

You must gear your mind up to get into the habit of doing what you need to do—NOW if your goal is to achieve at a very high level!

You can achieve untold success in your wealth-building future from this day forward, and a key component of that success is your willingness to take responsibility for your future in definite terms. You now have a real grasp of what you need to do (your responsibility) if you desire success at a high level, regardless of what stage you are at in your financial life!

Are you at this time disciplined enough to take responsibility for your and your family's future?

Now Is the Time for You to Truly Take Responsibility for Your Future

Even though you may not have caused your current situation, you must realize that it is your responsibility (how you got there is immaterial if you decide to take responsibility now) to respond appropriately and in a manner that truly benefits you and your family.

There is always a reason or excuse that you can give to explain your current situation and one that your mind and heart will accept if you allow it to happen.

However, until you take full responsibility for your current position and decide to take positive action to change your situation, you are operating in denial or fear!

By operating in denial, you are showing that you are not ready to change, and you are not ready to take control of your finances or any other area of your life where you are in denial!

By comprehending this book in a "sincere manner" at this time you are showing that you are not only ready to change, you are demonstrating a real determination to change your future and that of your family's in a major way!

The Art of Essential Action is a book for those who are "now ready" to change their future for the better in a major way and for those who have left excuses and blaming forces beyond their control for their current credit and finance position behind them!

This book is not for those who are in denial about their credit and finances, quite the contrary, **The Art of Essential Action** is a book created for those who know that they must take responsibility for their future and they want to take that responsibility in a manner that will take them to where they need or desire to be in the most efficient manner possible.

You can now utilize your mind in a responsible and meaningful way and in a way that can lead to you addressing your credit and finances in a comprehensive manner.

By doing so you reduce the stress in your and your family's life and you will make your and your family's years on planet earth a much more pleasurable experience and one where you can do more of what you prefer to do on a more consistent basis.

You will also rightfully take the responsibility that you were enshrined with at birth, to improve your and your family's net worth!

Chapter 4 Financially Alert Mind & Wealth Building

Learn the importance of being mentally alert—Financially Speaking...

Do you currently have:

Knowledge of your current circumstances or finances!

Inspiration to do more daily!

Commitment to do more daily!

Know that you don't know it all, but that's ok!

In this chapter you will learn if you need a KICK in the rear (metaphorically speaking) to do more so that you can not only soar, but also ROAR...

Do you take the right actions daily as it relates to your finances? Can you possibly do it better? It is important that you get on an "upward path" toward success with the management of your finances, where there is no turning back.

It is important that you realize that if you are lackadaisical or slow to act on financial matters in your life, you can change all that by adjusting your mind and changing your daily habits to achieve more.

You possess inside of you the ability to do much more on a daily basis, but it all starts with you knowing what you need to do on a daily basis, finding the inspiration within to want to do more, having the commitment to carry out what you need to do and knowing that you don't know it all, but there are places you can go to get the right or more helpful advice that can take you where you need or desire to be.

Starting today, make it a point to start knowing what you need to do on a daily basis in your financial life, make it a point to find the inspiration within to want to do more in your financial life, make it a point to have the commitment to carry out what you need to do in your financial life and have the inclination to know that you don't know all things—whether it be financial or otherwise, but the success that you desire can still be achieved!

You must know what is going on and what is really occurring in your financial life, if you are one who has a desire to achieve more and achieve optimally.

You must have a **comprehensive view** of what is occurring in your financial life, as that allows you to know "what is" going on, and "what needs to be" going on!

By living daily without a comprehensive plan of action, you put yourself in a vulnerable position with creditors and other financial operatives who may not have your best interest in mind—financially speaking.

Do you know your annual income and your annual debt? Do you know your monthly income and monthly debt? Do you know your monthly and annual discretionary income?

Do you know and understand your credit situation in a meaningful way?

Do you know all areas of your finances that you must address or are you like most and are at a loss to describe them?

Even if the required knowledge seems difficult or too much for you to comprehend at this time, you must get to a point where you have that knowledge and being able to use it to your advantage is almost second nature to you.

You must gain the inspiration to move to action on financial matters in your life that need to be acted upon if you truly desire to reach your goals in a timely manner. You must use the inspiration that you will receive to guide you toward gaining a solid financial foundation, and it all starts on the inside, by you having a high level of inspiration!

You must feel worthy of the success that you see coming once you know where you are headed. You must clearly see the path that you are on, and you must be inspired to act in the right manner—consistently.

You must always strive to do the best that is within you, and you must have the commitment within your mind and heart to consistently make the right moves, even if you are thrown off on occasion by unforeseen or unwanted circumstances occurring.

You must make it a habit to act immediately on what you know you need to do on a daily basis to make your dreams (goals) come true.

A real barometer of whether you are committed is whether you are putting your goals in writing that you know you want to achieve and having a measurable timetable for achieving the goals that you desire most.

By having a high level of commitment, you are showing that you are "apart from the crowd" and you are actively moving toward your goals with no excuses or distractions in front of you that will deter you along the way.

Even if you must take a detour due to unforeseen circumstances, your commitment level must remain high, and you must do what needs to be done!

You must also know what you don't know as far as your finances are concerned. Just testing your alertness—as in actuality, you can't know what you don't know, and you want to understand that we all have blind spots, and there are areas of finance that you may not know in-depth but that is ok.

No one knows it all as far as finances are concerned!

However, there is a large body of personal finance and wealth building knowledge, along with a number of ways **to successfully attack your finances** and achieve the goals that you desire that are readily prevalent and available from a vast array of sources.

A "comprehensive approach" will give you the solid financial foundation that you need to succeed and help you reach your goals in the most efficient manner possible throughout your lifetime. A "comprehensive approach" will help you see what you need to see so that you can effectively manage your finances and achieve many, if not all your financial goals.

Even with a comprehensive approach, you may not have the depth of knowledge in each area of your personal finances, but you will put yourself in position for success and you can get other professionals to work on your behalf from a position of strength—as opposed to putting yourself in position to be taken advantage of by having gaps in your financial understanding.

Don't kick yourself (no pun intended) if you are not achieving at the level that you desire at this time.

However, you want to know in definite terms that you control your future from this day forward!

You are responsible for knowing what needs to be done in your financial life to achieve at the level that you desire to be at—or at the level that you need to be at!

You are responsible for digging inside your mind and heart and finding new and more Inspiring ways to reach your goals!

You are responsible for having the daily commitment to stick to your written plans and really achieve in a timely manner!

You are responsible for knowing that there may be things that you don't know, yet you can still achieve positive results that will show!

The goal of this chapter is to put you in position to KICK toward the goalpost and make a winning field goal so that you can enjoy life on your terms.

You don't need a KICK in the rear—you now have the wake-up call that you need—to succeed!

You are now on a path to obtaining a "Financially Alert Mind" and "Financial Success!"

Now is the time that you give it your BEST and achieve major SUCCESS!

KICKstart your future—NOW!

Reading the material in this book on a consistent basis will show you HOW!

Learn How You Can Benefit Greatly by Having a Financially Alert Mind

You must realize that it is better to have a "financially alert mind" than to be "sleep at the wheel" as you journey towards your financial freedom!

Part of showing your love to your family and yourself is having a "Financially Alert Mind"—meaning you must know how to respond appropriately to all that happens in your financial life.

By being financially alert you will be of the mindset that you must act in a proactive manner as you move toward improving your credit and finances!

Those who have a financially alert mind know how to invest in a manner that serves their best long-term interests and they cannot be led astray by scammers and others who do not have their best interest in mind.

Personal Finance Sites that Can Further Help You Gain a Financially Alert Mind Include the Following:

Note: All the following are free sites or nominal rates—be sure to read the fine print and the terms of use. In addition, be sure to analyze each of the various websites to learn why having a **Financially Alert Mind** is so important!

Education:

1) www.realty-1-strategic-advisors.com

provides you the opportunity to gain the comprehensive preparation and knowledge that you need to succeed. It does so in an easy to understand and apply manner. It is a great site for those who desire to build a strong foundation as they manage their credit, financial and real estate affairs

Unlike other sites the mental aspect of credit and finance is looked at in a fresh and helpful manner

2) www.moneycrashers.com

provides an array of finance topics that you can benefit from and presents topics from a number of authors and sources

3) www.khanacademy.com

provides video and audio on saving, credit, budgeting and other financial topics and is a great site for those who like learning in an audio or video style

4) The Open University—https://www.open.edu/openlearn/money-business/retirement-planning-made-easy/content-section-0?active-tab=description-tab

provides personal finance course designed to educate you on personal finance and is a great course for those who like to learn in a course type format—includes many lessons—some that I am sure you can benefit from

5) MrMoneyMustache.com

provides those who desire to retire early or at least the option to retire early the opportunity to do so by living frugally, investing wisely and building wealth efficiently

6) TheWealthIncreaser.com

provides free reports on timely financial topics that can help you and your family increase your net worth in an intelligent, consistent and proactive manner

7) Investorship.com

provides a behavioral aspect to wealth building that can put you in more control of your finances

Saving:

1) www.Wepay.com—collects secure payments

2) MrMoneyMustache.com

3) Early Retirement & Wealth Building—TheWealthIncreaser.com/early-retirement-wealth-building/

Spending:

1) www.Viewpoints.com—strategic spending

Budgeting:

1) www.mint.com provides budgeting tools and other tools for those who want to effectively manage their finances—one of the best free budgeting sites available

2) TheWealthIncreaser.com provides wealth building and other tools for those who want to manage their finances. Financial products and other services offered for a stated fee

3) www.coupons.com great site for finding brand name coupon discounts

4) www.choosetosave.org helpful budgeting and saving site—particularly if you have excel on your computer (interactive budget)

5) www.thesmartassetbudgetcalculator helpful budget or cash flow calculator

Investing:

1) www.morningstar.com provides investment advice and research tools that are second to none

2) www.portfoliomonkey.com help in analyzing portfolios

3) www.kiplinger.com retirement planning calculator—and more

4) www.financialmentor.com free calculators for budgeting, mortgages and more—fee for various financial services

Real Estate:

1) www.the-best-atlanta-real-estate-advice.com provides real estate advice and information that home buyers and home sellers need to know. The content writer of www.realty-1-strategic-advisors.com is also the content writer of TheWealthIncreaser.com and the content is provided in a similar style

2) www.zillow.com provides home buyer and home seller information in markets across the United States

3) www.trulia.com a close competitor to zillow—they too provide home buyer and home seller information in markets across the United States

4) www.realtytrac.com foreclosure tracking site that provides data on communities across the United States

5) www.city-data.com provides helpful demographic data on communities in the United States

6) www.Neighborhoodscout.com—make affordable home move—and demographic data of interest

7) www.greatschools.com provides school rankings in communities across the United States

8) www.financialmentor.com/mortgagecalculators provides mortgage calculators to help you plan your future—and more

Other:

www.Annualcreditreport.com—all-in-one site for tracking your credit and obtaining your free credit reports from all three major credit bureaus

www.CharityNavigator.com—making smart donations

www.Kayak.com—booking cheap flights

www.Mytab.com—trip saving site

Expedia.com—compare and book hotel room while on vacation

www.HealthInReach.com—compare medical procedure costs

www.Socialpicks.com—share investment strategies

Why Having a "Financially Alert Mind" is so Important?

By gaining the knowledge that you need to succeed you put yourself in position to take your credit and financial success higher so that you can achieve the goals that you and your family desire.

By making a real commitment to use your mind in a **financially alert manner,** you can put yourself in position to achieve your and your family's financial mission!

By opening your mind up to what is possible you put yourself in control of your credit and finances and your future!

A **Financially Alert Mind** allows you to do your own thinking and allows you to "take action" on your own initiative and empowers you with the ability to achieve the goals that serve your and your family's best interest.

You won't have to be forced or inspired by others to act, you will act on your own initiative to create the future that you desire!

In a real sense that is what this book is all about, empowering you with the working knowledge that you need so that you can succeed!

Did you know that if you have the self-discipline, proper preparation, proper focus and the right knowledge that is necessary, you can manage many or all of the credit and financial affairs in your life and reach many or possibly all of your goals?

Always realize that if you can control your thought process and direct your actions the right way you can control your future!

You can choose to "build up" your future or "tear down" your future by your daily thoughts and by the actions that you take on a consistent basis!

Did you know that a **F**inancially **A**lert **M**ind **I**mproves **L**ives **Y**early?

By having a Financially Alert Mind you can put yourself and your family in position to reach many or all of your future goals that you desire and you can position yourself to attain the goals that can make a real difference in your and your family's life!

You can now show your LOVE to your family and benefit your **F A M I L Y** and yourself by having a Financially Alert Mind—this year!

As a result of purchasing this book, major success lies in your and your family's future. You can now sincerely pursue a path that will help you attain a financially alert mind in an efficient and highly effective way—today.

Chapter 5 Understanding Your Need to Act Consistently

Learn why a "consistent approach" will help you reach your goals faster...

It is important that you renew your mind daily! You may need to start fresh and you must expect success in your future on a **consistent basis!**

A **consistency** in approach allows you to know where you are going and will help provide you with the determination that you need to get there more efficiently!

Do you know what your goals and objectives are—and do you have a plan for achieving them? How can you attack your credit and finances more effectively? You **must have a system** that allows you to operate effectively in your daily finances on a **consistent** basis.

By consistently doing what is necessary, you put your heart and mind in position to achieve what you desire!

You now have a chance to learn what you need to do to attain **consistent** success!

The opportunity for you to achieve success on a **constant basis** is now in front of you! Are you at this time determined to do what you need to do? You must realize that to succeed **consistently** it may require the cooperation of others as no successful person is an island onto himself!

It is important that you focus on the important areas of your credit and finances so that you can gain a powerful advantage that will move you forward in an effective and efficient manner!

If you consistently do what you were put on earth to do, you can make your dreams come true!

You can never fail consistently if you decide to get up **consistently** and pursue success consistently!

By **consistently** looking inside yourself and improving on qualities or areas that you are weakest in—your weaker **and** stronger qualities will be greatly enhanced!

It is in your best interest to stay ahead of the curve than behind the curve! Did you know that to operate more effectively and efficiently, it requires **consistent action** on your part throughout your lifetime?

You must meet success head on and expect a collision with it—because success won't expect to find you and collide with you—if you don't do what you need to do!

You must realize that your consistent understanding of the material in this book alone is not enough! It is what you do with what you comprehend—and what you do with the knowledge that you will gain that really counts!

You must realize that in most cases something for nothing is usually worth nothing!

Don't get too excited about temporary success! You must diligently seek success on a permanent basis and put forward the required effort on a **consistent** basis!

Your "success consciousness" can be enhanced by not letting chaos and confusion distract you and send you in the opposite direction of success.

What quality and quantity of service do you provide to others on a **consistent** basis? The quality and quantity of service that you provide will determine in large part how successful you will be in your future!

If you earn consistently and save consistently you can start on a path to the success that you desire!

You must get to a point where the small voice within you that you hear speaks success, and you must expect nothing less than success **on a consistent basis!**

How high will you decide to go after you have faced great adversity? By having the right mindset, you can reach a higher level of success!

The longer your **consistent thought patterns** are, the greater your future success can be! What **you do consistently** determines in large part where you will go and how high you can take your success!

Are you happy where you are? Are you happy where you are going?

They are really one in the same! Once you line up your mind and heart with the goals that you desire to achieve, you make success much more likely to occur!

Your actions on a daily basis in large part determine your present and future success!

What are your aspirations? Do you desire financial freedom or just comfortable living—car—house—money in bank etcetera. Or, do you desire to leave a lasting legacy for your family and/or society?

Your **persistent and consistent** use of this book can provide you and your family a new look!

You can now put yourself in position to achieve untold success in your future by reading this book and comprehending the material at your highest level on a **consistent** basis!

Learn How You Can Use Inspiration to Reach Your Goals in a Timelier Manner

It is important that you are "inspired and have enthusiasm and vigor" while in the process of improving your credit and finances.

In these difficult times it can often be difficult to find the inspiration or strength to take positive action and get started on the process of improving your credit and finances in a major way!

You must visualize reaching and attaining your goals! There will be many obstacles that get in your path as you try to reach your goals.

The key point you must remember is that obstacles in your way are not uncommon when you are attempting to reach your financial goals!

It is important that you take positive action now if you feel inspired to do so. Many have felt motivated and inspired at a particular point in time, only to have the motivation and inspiration wither away and never to return.

Don't let that be you!

If you delay or procrastinate now you may never again feel as inspired as you are now!

If you take action now you will put in motion the power of positive momentum and your life will begin to take a change for the better.

There are many life events that have the potential to take away the inspiration that you feel now and the inspiration you feel now may never return again.

You must understand that inspiration is what will bring your future success into existence!

You will also have to "work" to make it happen, however your level of inspiration is the real key to making future success a real reality for you and your family!

By using the inspiration that you now feel, you can bring into existence the goals and objectives that you seek—if you make the decision to "act" on the inspiration that you now feel!

You must be inspired, and you must realize in your mind what you want to accomplish in your credit and financial life.

Once you sincerely realize "in your mind" what you really want to occur in your credit and financial life and you make the commitment that is necessary—the success that you desire will happen for you and your family!

Even in my own life I was highly inspired to create the best websites (which was a daunting task) on the web for consumers who were seeking real estate and financial improvement advice.

Despite being highly motivated and inspired I too had numerous life events that set me back and made the task more difficult. There were times when I felt disheartened and less inspired after being stung by a bee for two months in a row and going into anaphylactic shock and almost losing my life.

In the subsequent month my lower back went out and I was in severe pain for weeks.

However, my faith and inspiration was and is so strong that no obstacle would prevent the goals that were set for realty-1-strategic-advisors.com and the-best-atlanta-real-estate-advice.com from not coming into fruition.

I had already conceived (visualized) the sites and believed in my heart (set goals) that it would occur—and after several years it occurred.

E-mails and conversations from around the world attest to the real estate and personal finance improvement of consumers on a constant basis, which was the original goal of both sites.

It is important that you get started on a serious path to credit and finance improvement today!

I leave you with a poem that I became inspired to create after I was faced with an impending feeling of death after I went into anaphylactic shock after being stung by a bee.

Even so, I knew that death would not occur based on my faith!

Hopefully you will find some inspiration in this poem to take positive action now and improve the credit and finance position of yourself, your family and others who are of concern to you—for years to come.

THE STRENGTH TO SUCCEED IS WITHIN YOU

Lord give me the strength to do all that I need to do?

You know I will give all the glory to you!

It is you who have empowered me to be all that I can be!

When I think back and analyze all my accomplishments—it is you whom I see!

Guide me and lead me to do what is right—for I know you will, you have always shined your bright light!

Be with me every step of the way!

Strengthen me so my convictions will not sway!

I give my thanks to you on this day!

Continue to give me the ability to change lives in a positive way!

In life, obstacles will always cross your path, and it is how you respond to them that will determine your success or failure on a constant basis!

Your Need to Cultivate the Habit of Positive Thinking

You must believe in your heart and mind that you can accomplish any goal that you visualize and take action toward achieving.

In short—no excuse will do as you must operate daily with confidence Starting today, use the control of your mind and thought process to get started on improving your finances and living conditions for you and your family.

You must stay inspired and never lose your enthusiasm for improving your credit and finance position.

A proactive approach to managing your finances can lead to greater success during your lifetime.

It is important that you realize that you don't have to suffer or make the same mistakes that others make if you do what you need to do at this time.

Even if you have managed your credit and finances poorly, you can put yourself in position for future success if you decide right now to take the necessary action on the front end!

You can now approach your credit and finances in a proactive manner by putting into action the concepts in this book, as many of the concepts have already made a major impact in the lives of money managers around the world.

However, it is important that you come to your own conclusion and **The Art of Essential Action** provides you the opportunity to do just that.

Also realize that only a select few "want" to move forward in a proactive manner and take the management of their credit and finances to a very high level to really benefit themselves and their family as many will comprehend the material, but only a small percentage will apply the information in a way that will transform their life!

Are you one of the select few or are you unsure of what you want to do?

Only those who are proactive (or willing to be proactive by gaining the qualities that are needed) and sincerely want to put in the required effort to make their dreams a reality will attain the success that they desire or need to attain.

Isn't it time that you take a proactive approach and do what is best for yourself and your family?

You don't have to blame others, outside forces or make excuses because you have not achieved at the level that you desire to achieve at.

By starting today, a better future for you and your family can definitely be on the way!

Over the years it has been discovered that consumers who receive good input (knowledge) on a regular basis on the front-end (proactively) are generally able to reach their highest potential when managing and improving their credit and finances, as compared to those who don't.

Isn't it time that you use a smarter, more proactive approach to attacking your credit and finances?

Isn't it time that you achieve what you desire so that you can take your living standards higher?

You can now do so if you choose to!

You can now put yourself in position to make your dreams come true if you do what you need to do!

You can make it happen now—and **The Art of Essential Action** will show you how!

You must be willing to give it "your" best as you pursue a new level of success.

It is important that you renew your mind daily! You may need to start fresh and you must expect success in your future on a **consistent basis!**

In the remainder of this chapter you will take a deeper dive into how you can use your mind and your ability to act to achieve more. Furthermore, you will learn ways that you can **make more of an impact toward achieving your wealth building goals** so that you can "have a real opportunity" to achieve more in less time and live more abundantly from this day forward.

- **You must have a yearning to make an impact as it relates to your finances**

In life we all have ambitions or goals that we want to achieve, and as far as financial planning is concerned, those ambitions or goals can be numerous.

You want to have an attitude of always reaching higher so that you can reach the goals that you desire. By reaching higher you can operate at a higher level of excellence, (pun intended) and you can do so at this time if you are fully committed **and** you know the actions that you need to complete as you can now move to a new beat, if you are now ready to move to action appropriately so that it is the goals that you desire that you meet!

- **You must know the action steps that you need to take to make a real impact**

The reason most people fail to achieve or reach many of their financial goals are that they often don't know what steps they need to take to make it happen—or more importantly make it happen in as efficient a manner as possible.

You will soon be in position to avoid this pitfall that has hampered many over the years. By setting meaningful goals and knowing the right steps to take to move toward achieving those goals you are properly preparing your heart and mind up for operating at a **higher level** of excellence and putting yourself in position to reach those significant goals!

By focusing on **"the alphabets below"**—you can learn steps that you can take **right now** so that you can get started on operating daily at "peak performance" and achieve results that will show—so that you can better utilize information that will put you in the know.

A--Cash Flow Analysis

B—Credit Analysis

C—Comprehensive Financial Analysis

- **You must put into action on a consistent basis the steps that will take you toward your goals with more impact**

Your application of the steps mentioned above in a manner that is germane to your and your family's financial future and most important goals are what will help you attain your goals in a more efficient manner

By doing what needs to be done to help improve your finances you are showing discipline and a real desire to reach the goals that you are motivated to achieve.

By taking "impactful action steps" on a consistent basis, you are showing that you truly believe, thereby setting yourself up for the success that you will soon achieve.

Isn't it time you listen appropriately to your inner voice, learn more as it relates to effective money management that can lead to you reaching many, if not all your goals so that you can show your true love to your family and others whom you associate with?

Isn't it time you travel down a "road to success" that has fewer twists and turns–and know in more definite terms that narrow is the path that you travel, and abundance is the destination that you seek?

It is important that you plan on aggressively attacking your finances and you operate "impactfully" so that you won't suffer from insecurity as you climb higher and higher towards what you truly desire.

When it comes to operating at a high level, you want to make sure that the work that you put in proactively has a "real impact" as you must know at all times that ***it is you*** *who must want to do so and it is you who MUST say GO!*

You must be sincere in your desire to make a real impact on your finances and life in a better way, and if you are—you will pursue your wealth building goals with a higher level of commitment. Starting today you can get momentum going your way and achieve lasting results that are here to stay! In summary, to achieve at a level that will **make a real impact** you must have the desire to **ignite your own fire inside** so that when you achieve your goals, you can glide, and when you land you will know that you truly enjoyed your ride.

At all times you must realize that you control your destiny and the **direction that you can take** in your life. Now is the time that you not only realize that, but you put action plans into effect so that you can achieve more and improve your score.

Did you know that you are:

Chosen by God to be anxious for nothing

Chosen by God to know that your daily thoughts mean something

Chosen by God to not be negatively stressed

Chosen by God to not operate with less

Chosen by God not to be a mess

Chosen by God to give it your very best

Adequately blessed by God to pass any test

It is important that you operate as "impactfully" as you can, and pursue unlimited wealth building and overall success as you give it your absolute best.

It is also important that you use all of the appropriate tools that are at your disposal to **move toward your goals** with **more of a winning attitude,** so that you can pursue your goals in a better mood.

And in a similar manner as the concept of **A-B-C**, mentioned earlier in this chapter, **C3 & Me©** is a short acronym for **what you need to do** to get started on a path toward making your dreams come true, and more importantly allows you to see your finances from the right view.

Cash Flow Analysis, **C**redit Analysis, **C**omprehensive Financial Analysis or **C3** for short, can get you started on a more definite path toward wealth building success, if you are **at this time**, willing to give it your absolute best.

1–-**C**ash Flow Analysis

2—**C**redit Analysis

3—**C**omprehensive Financial Analysis

By taking the **3 steps above** to heart and having a **sincere desire** to **do your part** on a more **consistent basis**, you can take your mind to new places and move about **throughout your life** at the right paces.

Your ability to achieve more in these tumultuous times are contingent upon you having a **mindset of resilience** on a daily basis.

Your goal is to be **well grounded** and **not puzzled** by what is in front of you financially and in all areas of your life.

From this day forward you must always know that:

You are responsible for doing your **C**ash flow analysis so that you can at a minimum know your inflow and outflow of cash on a monthly basis which can provide you the needed direction to make the necessary adjustments and win the majority of your races!

You are responsible for doing **C**redit analysis so that you can at a minimum know the five credit factors that you must know and learn in detail how you can use those factors to your advantage throughout your lifetime!

You are responsible for doing a **C**omprehensive analysis of your overall finances so that you can at a minimum know what–and how to address your insurance, investments, taxes, emergency fund, education planning, estate planning/wills and retirement planning so that your building of wealth is enhanced in a real and meaningful way–so that the wealth that YOU accumulate is more likely to be here to stay!

By **integrating the three concepts** that you have learned, you can **transform your mind** and the **path that you can take** during good times or tough times throughout your lifetime so that you can do your part to help ensure a more prosperous future for you and your loved ones, based in large part on the actions that **YOU** took to create your new look!

C3 & Me© can now take you to places that you need to be!

Conclusion or Key Points

In the same manner as the author of **The Art of Essential Action** was chosen by God to pursue and achieve goals that are not odd—so too can you use the inspiration that you receive to pursue the goals that you perceive and the goals that you were meant to receive, to make something big happen in your life—as you too are chosen by God to **DO MORE** and reach higher as you pursue your life purpose and other goals that you desire!

Isn't it time that you become **more proficient** and **more consistent** in the management of your finances?

In the coming years and beyond, you don't have to live in strife if you at this time decide to take control of your financial life!

Although achieving your goals are not as easy as **A-B-C** or **1-2-3,** those goals that you really want to achieve can be conceptualized and brought into existence by you in a relatively straight-forward and time efficient manner if you apply the right approach.

*However, it is your responsibility to **expend the needed effort** to **put together a plan** that can lead to lasting success for you and your family throughout your lifetime.*

It is important that you approach your wealth building efforts with confidence regardless of the season or environment that you operate in.

Always realize that inspiration often comes down and doesn't make a sound, however you know that it is around because you will move to action, as the spirit in you to "move-to-action" will abound!

The ability to do great things resides inside of you, and you must tap into what it is that can lead you toward making your dreams come true.

By **C**ontrolling Your **A**ctions **N**ow you **can** position yourself for a lifetime of success if you are sincerely willing to give it your absolute best.

As you gear up your mind and heart to roam, the time is again right to leave you with a poem:

God Gives Me Strength

God gives me the strength to do what I need to do to make my dreams come true

Out of all that is happening to me now, God continues to show me how

As I reflect on my current state of affairs, God continues to show me the right steps to take as I climb the stairs

My vision of the steps that I need to take has been made clear to me

By giving it my absolute best and pursuing my goals at my highest level, I know that I can be who "I" want to be

God has provided me the strength that I need, in large part because I made "a real" commitment to succeed

You must give it your best by acting consistently, utilizing your **A-B-C** knowledge, **C3 success** and living daily at a level that allows you to pass any test!

You no longer have to **hesitate or wait** and achieve your goals at a time that is late, if you make the decision to pursue more on this date! Also, be sure to use humor and laughter as a major tool as you build wealth as that approach will play a major role in improving your mental health and living daily with joy on the inside!

Always remember that nothing that you face in life is too hot to handle or too cold to hold! Your goal is to get more income, cut expenses or do a combination of the two, if that is something that you need to do, and you are sincere about making your dreams come true.

If you are now in a position where you have adequate **discretionary income**, you can put a plan in place that will allow you to attain your retirement and other goals so that you can continue to live at the level that you are currently living at—or a higher level if you plan now to make it all happen.

You want to learn at an early point in your wealth building journey that there could possibly be a better way for you to travel towards your goals on this day!

You must do what is necessary to get moving toward what you need to make happen to create the right atmosphere and bring more into your life that is rewarding and uplifting while you are here on planet earth.

Additionally, you must do so knowing your self-worth and have a sincere yearning to reach higher and definitely utilize the gifts that you were given at birth!

All the best as you make a **major impact toward building true wealth**, and use consistency in action to put procrastination to rest, as you get your life back on track, as you are now, or soon will be, in position to more aggressively attack.

Chapter 6 Hot Time Management & Action Topics (understanding compounding, income, inflation, how to increase your net worth and improving your credit and finance management)

Learn how you can benefit from the use of compounding and understanding the various types of income among other concerns...

Over the past several years we have had an increase in the number of questions regarding the topic of compounding, income, inflation, how to increase your net worth and other concerns—and in this chapter we will address those topics and how you can use the knowledge gained to achieve the goals that will serve your and your family's best long-term interests.

What Exactly is Compounding?

First and foremost, it is important that you realize that interest is either:

1) Simple, or
2) Compound

SIMPLE INTEREST:

Simple Interest is a quick method of calculating the interest charge on a loan or the interest that will be earned on an investment.

Simple interest is determined by multiplying the interest rate by the principal—by the number of periods.

Simple interest is quite easy to understand as it is simply calculated as follows:

$1,000 at 7% interest is equal to $70 dollars in interest on an annual basis!

Over a 20-year period with simple interest you would accumulate ($70 times 20 years) $1,400!

Now let's look at COMPOUNDING...

Compound interest is when interest is added to the principal of a deposit, investment or loan, so that, from that moment on, **the interest that has been added** also earns interest.

Compound interest is often misunderstood by many, and it is calculated as follows (you need a financial calculator to compute):

$1,000 compounded annually at 7% for 20 years and you were to reinvest the interest, you would accumulate roughly $3,870—a difference of ($3,870 minus $1,400) $2,570 from the "simple interest" that you would receive over the same 20-year time period!

Now let's look at <u>$10,000</u> invested over a 20-year period at 7% interest using both SIMPLE and COMPOUND Interest!

$10,000 at 7% interest is equal to $700 dollars in interest with simple interest on an annual basis and over a 20-year period you would accumulate $14,000!

$10,000 compounded annually at 7% for 20 years and you were to reinvest the interest you would accumulate roughly $38,700—a difference of ($38,700 minus $14,000) $24,700 over a 20-year period!

Now you get the picture...

If the above returns were inside of your retirement account such as an IRA, 457, 403b, Thrift Savings Plan or 401k—no taxes would be due on an annual basis (you can have the following inside of your retirement account(s) among others): bank CD, Money Market Account, Bond Fund, Stocks, or Mutual Fund(s) etcetera.

If the above returns were outside of your retirement account such as in a bank CD, Money Market Account, Bond Fund, Stocks, or Mutual Fund etcetera, taxes would be due on an annual basis. Interest, dividends and capital gains would possibly be taxable.

Your emergency fund balance would be considered "outside of your retirement account" and the interest earned would be taxable on a yearly basis, however with savings and money market interest rates often low at times, the taxes would be very low. If the interest rates in accounts that you have "outside of your retirement accounts" rises or you have capital gains, you would be taxed on the interest or gain at your ordinary income or capital gains rate.

The key point to remember is that your money will grow at a faster rate if left untouched and the interest is compounded over time!

If you continue to add money to the investment over time your returns will be even larger over time!

Therefore, as part of your long-term strategy, you must come up with ways that you can invest both "inside and outside" of your retirement accounts at a level that will take you to where you need or want to be during your retirement years and beyond.

All of that sounds great you say—but where will I find the money to invest over a number of years, I barely have enough to live on?

You must first determine where you are financially by doing the following at a minimum:

1) You must have a system in place to determine your monthly cash flow so that you will know the amount of your discretionary income on a monthly basis.

2) You must put a plan in place to reduce or eliminate your outstanding debt (know money saving moves that you can make) and you may have to come up with a plan to get additional income and/or reduce your monthly expenses, or do a combination of the two.

3) You must properly establish an emergency fund.

4) You must properly analyze and address all areas of your finances.

If you can come up with a way to get just an additional $80 or so a month after or while you have addressed the above—after a 20-year period at 7% interest compounded monthly, you could have over $40,000 in those account(s)!

If you could come up with a way to get an additional $800 per month—after 20 years at 7% interest compounded monthly, you could have over $400,000 in the account(s).

If the investments were inside a ROTH IRA you would be able to withdraw the contributions tax free at any time—as taxes on the "contributions" have already been paid. If over 59 ½, you could withdraw the contributions and earnings tax free (certain restrictions apply) or let the account continue to grow as there are no mandatory withdrawals with a ROTH IRA.

If the contributions were made to a Traditional IRA you could deduct the contributions on your taxes on a yearly basis up to a limit (certain restrictions apply).

Once you withdrew the contributions and earnings during your retirement years you pay taxes (you would normally be in a lower tax bracket) after age 59 ½.

If you withdrew early (before age 59 ½) there would be taxes on withdrawal and a 10% early withdrawal penalty unless an exception was applicable.

If you have a family of 5 you could possibly save $80 or so on a monthly basis by going to coupons.com and smartsource.com and use coupons on items you normally buy and possibly save $80 or more per month.

You could possibly cut your energy costs by changing over to fluorescent light bulbs, installing an electronic setback thermostat, sealing air pockets in your home, sealing gaps in your home with insulation, cutting back on monthly entertainment, insulating your hot water pipes, reducing or cutting back on your internet/tv, ending monthly subscriptions—and by making any of those moves or taking any of those actions, you could possibly free up an additional $80 or so per month.

The opportunities for coming up with additional revenue are unlimited and you must use your imagination and your creativity to come up with more income or reduce your current monthly expenses on a consistent basis (or more likely, do a combination of the two)!

OK—Let's Recap...

Compounding is one of the simplest and least painful ways that you can utilize to help you reach your future goals in a more time efficient manner.

The key is to get yourself and your family in a "favorable financial position" by addressing your credit and finances in a critical manner on the front end or proactively.

Once you do that you can position yourself and your family properly so that you can invest in your future in a manner that can be of greater benefit!

Whether you are investing inside or outside of your retirement accounts you want to be in position to use the power of compounding to your and your family's best advantage.

Always realize that you may have to get additional income and/or cut your expenses to achieve your desired goals!

When you invest, you must be conscious of what is occurring! When an investment earns interest or dividends, your total amount invested increases.

That increased amount earns even more interest or compounds (if left alone) and the cycle continues if you don't pull out cash.

Be sure that you know the compounding frequency, the more frequent the compounding, the more you will earn!

Monthly compounding is better than quarterly! Daily compounding is better than monthly and so on!

If you invest on a continuous basis and/or increase the amount, the growth rate will be even more than if you did not do so!

Keep in mind that certain types of investments could lose value (stocks, bonds, mutual funds etcetera)—that is why it is important that you know how to invest in a manner that serves your and your family's best long-term interest (you must know the risk, time-horizon and other factors that may be unique to you and your family).

You must also realize that inflation will always raise its ugly head, therefore be sure to factor that in as your buying power will be negatively affected over time.

You can achieve untold success in your future and if you are truly determined, you will find a way to make compounding work for you and your family—not against (creditor's use of compounding to their benefit due to your unwise use of credit) you and your family!

It is important that you realize that credit card companies, consumer lending companies and other creditors use compounding to their benefit and to your detriment. Therefore if you currently have credit card or other outstanding debt, you must come up with a plan to reduce or eliminate that debt now!

Doing so at this time will put you and your family on a positive path to making compounding work for you, and will move you and your family in the direction where—success lives!

In addition to understanding how compound interest works, you must also have "Working Knowledge of the Various Types" of income.

Understanding the Various Types of Income

Over the years we have found that consumers are often confused by the different types of income that they hear or read about.

In the remainder of this chapter, you can put yourself in position to remove the confusion that you may have about the **various types of income** that you may hear or read about during the various phases of your life by comprehending the material at your highest level.

Active Income

Active Income is Earned Income. When you perform a service for payment in the form of salary, wages, commissions, or tips, you're earning "active" income.

Also, if you actively manage rental real estate, you will have "active income" that could be advantageous to you from a tax perspective.

Adjusted Gross Income

Adjusted Gross Income or **(AGI)** as it is often called is used in the United States (and other Countries) on individual income tax returns and it represents the total gross income that you earn for the year—minus certain deductions and is calculated on page 1 of IRS form 1040.

Taxable Income is adjusted gross income less allowances for adjustments, credits, exemptions and itemized deductions and **taxable income is the last entry on page 1** of IRS form 1040.

Taxable Income will be explained in greater detail later in this chapter.

For most consumers who file a U.S., individual tax return AGI is more relevant than gross income.

Gross income is income that you receive from all sources and includes sales price of goods or property, less cost of the property sold, plus other income.

Gross Income includes wages, interest, dividends, business income, rental income, and all other types of income that you may receive.

Contrast with **Adjusted Gross Income** which is income that you receive for the year—less deductions.

Several deductions (e.g. medical expenses and miscellaneous itemized deductions) are limited based on a percentage of AGI. Certain phase outs, including those of lower tax rates and itemized deductions, are based on levels of AGI.

Many states base state income tax on AGI with certain deductions, therefore you want to select a tax professional who understands this—and can use that understanding for your greater benefit.

After-Tax Income

The amount of money that you have left over after all federal, state and withholding taxes have been deducted from your taxable income equals your after-tax income.

After-tax income represents the amount of "disposable income" that you have to spend on future investments or on current consumption.

After-Tax Income is often called “income after taxes” or disposable income.

When analyzing or forecasting your personal cash flows (or budget and personal income statement), it is important to use an estimated after-tax net cash flow or your disposable income so that you can get a real feel of where you are financially.

This is a more appropriate measure because your after-tax cash flows are what you actually have available for consumption.

This is not to say that all of your investments are purchased with after tax income—some companies offer salary deferral retirement plans that deduct money on a pre-tax basis (401ks, Thrift Plans, 457, 403bs etcetera).

The money invested on a "pre-tax basis" would not be taxed immediately (benefit to you) but instead would be taxed once you decided to withdraw the funds (such as during your retirement years).

However, because most people have less income during their retirement years compared to their prime earning years, the amount of tax paid would normally be less.

Discretionary Income

Discretionary Income is the money that you would have remaining after all your bills are paid off on a monthly or yearly basis.

It is income after subtracting taxes and your normal expenses!

Your monthly expenses such as rent or mortgage, utilities, insurance, medical, transportation, property maintenance, child support, inflation, food and other miscellaneous monthly expenses that you pay to maintain a certain standard of living that you desire for yourself and your family would all be paid from your disposable income—and what would be left over is your discretionary income.

Discretionary Income is the amount of your income available for spending after the essentials (such as food, clothing, and shelter) have been taken care of on a monthly or annual basis.

To derive your discretionary income, you would take your gross income *and subtract* your taxes and necessities on a monthly or annual basis.

"Disposable Income" is often incorrectly used to denote discretionary income—therefore, it is important that you are able to distinguish between the two in your mind from the context in which it is spoken or written.

The meaning and your understanding of disposable income and discretionary income should be interpreted from the context in which it is spoken or written and not merely on what is communicated.

"Disposable Income" is the amount of **money you have left after the payment** of your "taxes" left to spend or save.

When applying for a loan (mortgage, consumer loan), lenders may take into consideration your discretionary income to assess your loan repayment capacity.

Discretionary Income provides the lender with more information on your capacity to repay than the debt-to-income ratio in the case where you have a lot of debt.

In some cases, potential borrowers may have a lot of income, such that the percentage of available income may be smaller than normal standards would allow, but the actual amount of money is still large and would support a loan that the borrower is requesting.

Always distinguish in your mind that "discretionary income" is the amount of your income that is left for spending, investing or saving **after** your "taxes and personal necessities" (such as food, shelter, and clothing) have been paid.

It is money that "you" have "discretion over" as to how you want to utilize it (spend or save)!

Discretionary income includes money spent on luxury items, vacations, savings and non-essential goods and services.

Discretionary Income is “derived from” disposable income, which equals gross income minus taxes.

The total discretionary income levels for an economy will fluctuate over time, typically in line with business cycle activity—and "discretionary income" on an individual or family basis will also fluctuate over time based on household income and expense changes.

When economic output is strong (as measured by GDP or other market indicators), discretionary income levels tend to be high as well.

Or another way of looking at it is when the economy is booming discretionary income will tend to be higher.

On an individual basis if you were to get a raise at your job, cut expenses or work a secondary job—your "discretionary income" would normally increase, unless you were deficit spending on a monthly basis.
If inflation occurs in the price of life's necessities, then your discretionary income will fall, assuming that your wages, your expenses and your taxes remain constant or relatively constant.

Discretionary spending is an important part of a healthy economy. People will only spend money on things like travel, movies, entertainment and consumer electronics if they have the funds to do so.

Some people will use credit cards to purchase discretionary goods, but increasing personal debt is not the same as having discretionary income.

And using credit unwisely can be a dangerous strategy as it is possible that you could run your credit balance up to a level where it would be difficult or impossible to repay in a manner that made good financial sense.

Disposable Income

It is important that you distinguish in your mind that Disposable Income is money that you have left after paying your taxes—while discretionary income is money that you have left over after paying your taxes "and" mortgage/rent, food, utilities, and life's other necessities.

Disposable Income is the amount of money that you and/or your household have available for spending and saving after income taxes have been accounted for.

Disposable Personal Income is often monitored as one of the many "key economic indicators" used to gauge the overall state of the economy, and it is calculated as follows:

Disposable Personal Income versus Discretionary Personal Income

If you earn $100,000 and were in the 28% tax bracket your "disposable income" would be $72,000 on an annual basis.

Let's say you have yearly household expenses of $40,000—your "discretionary income" would be $32,000 on an annual basis.

On a monthly basis your disposable and discretionary income would be as follows:

On a monthly basis your earnings would be $8,333 and your taxes would be $2,333, leaving you with a disposable income of $6,000.

With monthly expenses of $3,333 per month your discretionary income ($8,333 minus $2,333 minus $3,333) would be $2,667 monthly.

Be sure to understand the two examples above as by doing so you will be in position to understand disposable and discretionary income in clear terms!

NOTE: *State and possibly local taxes have not been taken into consideration in the above example.*

In 2005, the average **disposable personal income** dipped into negative territory for the first time since 1933.

This means that in 2005, Americans were spending their entire DPI or Disposable Personal Income—and then tapping into debt for further spending.

Do your best to avoid that scenario in your and your family's credit and financial life!

The disposable income per capita in the United States was over $60,000 according to many market watchers. Keep in mind the average number notably does not reflect the gap between the richest and the rest of society, as the gap is substantial.

Gross Income

Gross Income is your total personal income before taking taxes or deductions into account.

Your gross income is how much you make before taxes. Gross Income is the figure people are looking for when they ask you how much you gross a month or year.

Gross Income is an important number when analyzing your personal finances, it indicates how you could more effectively plan your and your family's credit and financial future.

Keep in mind that gross income varies widely from individual to individual.

You must always remember that "Gross Income" is all your income from taxable sources, before subtracting any adjustments, deductions or credits.

Be able to contrast that with Net Income which is your income after subtracting any adjustments, deductions or credits.

Investment or Portfolio Income

You must know that investment income includes income that you earn from savings and checking accounts, dividends from stock purchases and ETFs, Mutual Funds and other market investments that are in many cases taxable.

If inside of your retirement account or otherwise excepted from taxation the income would generally be taxable.

Modified Adjusted Gross Income

Certain tax calculations are based on modified versions of AGI.

The definition of Modified Adjusted Gross Income (MAGI) varies according to the purpose for which it is used.

These modified versions may add certain items to AGI that were excluded in computing gross income. Common additions include tax exempt interest and the excluded portion of Social Security benefits.

Modified Adjusted Gross Income or MAGI is often used when calculating the alternative minimum tax (AMT).

Net Income

Simply put, income is defined as money that comes into your personal household, usually generated as compensation in the form of a paycheck for work you and other household members have done.

Net income refers to take home pay, or the amount of money earned after payroll withholding such as state and federal income taxes, social security taxes, and pretax benefits like health insurance premiums.

If you are enrolled in a flexible spending account to pay for medical costs, the amount withheld from each check is also on a pre-tax basis.

Always realize that you save on your taxes when you pay for benefits on a pre-tax basis and if used effectively you can build a large nest egg that will allow you to enjoy retirement in a way that it was meant to be enjoyed.

If your employer matches your retirement contributions, be sure to contribute at least up to the match and even more if your financial position allows you to do so.

By doing the above you can put yourself in position to live your retirement in a manner that you desire—not in a manner that others desire that you live!

To maximize your retirement returns be sure to start early in your life stage and be sure to put a plan in place that allows you to reach your "retirement number" that you need to reach so that you can enjoy retirement on your terms!

In simple form Net Income is Gross Income *less* Deductions!

Net Income also includes other sources of income that you may have from rideshare driving, selling goods or services by doing a side job, getting paid for consulting services or selling products you've made or are reselling on eBay/Amazon, your own website, at art and craft shows or other venues.

Another form of income is passive income, which is generated when you rent out rooms, homes or apartments, or you earn capital gains, interest or dividends on investments or interest bearing accounts like savings accounts or some checking accounts.

Other types of income come from royalties, which are gained from agreements made relating to copyrights, patents, or gas, mineral or petroleum properties.

Believe it or not even bartering can be a way of generating income, if you strike a really good deal.

It is not uncommon for consumers to pursue multiple streams of income based on the times that we now live in.

If you are computer savvy you can track your personal finances on software, like Quicken or you can go online to mint.com or a vast array of new online players that have financial platforms.

Other helpful links that could help you improve your personal finances and income can be found by visiting TheWealthIncreaser.com website.

Ordinary Income

Ordinary income is income that is categorized for tax purposes as being taxed in the category that your income level falls based on your filing status.

Ordinary Income will vary from individual to individual and family to family based on the income that you earned during a tax year.

Ordinary income is any type of income earned by an organization or individual that is taxable at ordinary rates, *such as wages, salaries, tips, interest income from* bonds *and commissions.*

It is important that you contrast ordinary income with long-term capital gains, the rise in the value of investments owned for more than a year, and qualified dividends which are both taxed differently and are therefore not considered to be ordinary income and may receive a more favorable tax treatment depending on your income—so you must be aware of ordinary income and the role that it plays now, or the role that it could play in your future.

Ordinary Income comes in two forms:

1) business income and

2) personal income

In a corporate setting, the term refers to any type of income generated from regular day to day business operations, excluding any income earned from the sale of long-term capital assets, such as land or equipment.

Meanwhile, from a personal perspective, ordinary income can be defined as any sort of cash inflow that is subject to income tax, as outlined by the Internal Revenue Service (IRS).

In a nutshell "ordinary income" is any type of income that is taxable at ordinary rates—according to IRS guidelines.

Passive Income

If you were to collect income from a business venture in which you're not actively involved, you're passively earning income. This could include income from rental properties that you may own and investment returns.

There are tax advantages and disadvantages of having passive income and each taxpayer's situation will differ.

Personal Income

Personal income is also known as your "before-tax income" and is used in calculating your adjusted gross income for income-tax purposes.

Personal Income is basically your "Gross Income" that was discussed earlier. It is your total income before taxes or any deductions and can include various sources.

Tariffs

Although not a type of income, tariffs often cause an increase in prices for many products and can have a negative effect on your disposable and discretionary income.

In the spring of 2025 "tariffs" became a very popular topic around the world as tariff (trade) wars were created and many countries around the world were involved.

Effective tariff policy requires serious study, analysis, foresight and planned negotiation—and if done appropriately can be an effective tool in managing trade more advantageously.

Tariffs are tax paid on imported goods by importers, and companies normally pass this and other taxes along to the consumer to maintain their profit margins and stay in business.

You want to know how tariffs will affect you and your family and plan accordingly.

Taxable Income

Taxable Income is a tax that governments impose on financial income generated by all entities or individuals within their jurisdiction.

By law, businesses and individuals generally must file an income tax return every year to determine whether they owe any taxes or are eligible for a tax refund.

Personal Taxable Income is derived by including all taxable income sources and subtracting out adjustments, exclusions, deductions and credits to determine your taxable income.

You must be able to distinguish between a tax credit and a tax deduction!

It is important that you realize that a tax "credit" reduces your tax dollar for dollar!

For example, if you owed $3,000 on your taxes and you were in the 25% tax bracket and you had a tax credit of $1,000—your taxes would then be reduced to $2,000!

A tax "deduction" would also reduce your taxes, however it would not be dollar for dollar—but would depend on your tax bracket!

For example, if you owed taxes of $3,000 and you were in the 25% tax bracket and you had a tax deduction of $1,000, your taxes would then be reduced to $2,750 (.25 times $1,000)!

The point is that a credit is more valuable to you than a tax deduction—so always keep that in mind!

You must properly purchase your home, and you must properly understand housing ratios!

Keeping your housing ratio under 30% and your housing and debt ratio under 40% of your monthly income are a wise use of benchmarks.

If your take home pay (or gross income) is $10,000 per month, your maximum mortgage payment should be $3,000.

$3,000/$10,000 = .30

or 30% on the front-end housing ratio (monthly housing payment only *versus* your monthly income)

If you have monthly recurring debt of 1 year or more such as monthly credit card debt of $500, monthly car payment of $500 and student loan debt of $1,000—your housing and debt ratio would be at 50% which in many cases would signify you had "too much" debt.

$5,000/$10,000 = .50

or 50% on the back-end housing ratio (monthly housing payment plus your monthly debt payments of 1 year or more *versus* your monthly income)

Keep in mind that compensating factors and extenuating circumstances (expected financial windfall, better school district for your kids—etcetera) could make it possible for you to *have a need* to exceed the above benchmarks, however use caution!

In addition, you must ensure that your discretionary income (mentioned earlier in this chapter) is at an acceptable level so that you can live the lifestyle that you desire for yourself and your family.

If you were to eliminate your student loan debt of $1,000 per month prior to purchasing your home—using the above scenario your housing and debt ratio drops down to the more acceptable benchmark area of 40%—now you get the picture?

$4,000/$10,000 = .40 or

40% on the back-end housing ratio (monthly housing payment plus your monthly debt payments of 1 year or more *versus* your monthly income).

Income tax is a key source of funds that the government (local, state, federal) use to fund its activities and serve the public.

Most countries employ a **progressive income tax system** in which higher income earners pay a higher tax rate compared to their lower earning counterparts.

That is the case in the United States as well!

The first income tax imposed in America was during the War of 1812 and its original purpose was to fund the repayment of a $100 million debt that was incurred through war-related expenses.

After the war, the tax was repealed, but income tax in the United States became permanent during the early 1900's.

What it all Means in a Practical Sense

Understanding the various types of income that you may hear or read about from various sources daily or on occasion can be difficult to decipher if you do not have a mental system to distinguish effectively among the various types.

Below we will review what you have just learned to further increase your understanding.

• You now know that your Adjusted Gross Income represents the total gross income that you earn for the year minus certain deductions.

• You now know that your After-Tax Income represents the amount of money that you have left over after all federal, state and withholding taxes have been deducted from your taxable income.

After-Tax Income is the same as "disposable income" so be aware of the interchanging use of the terms.

• You now know that your Discretionary Income represents the money that you would have remaining after all your bills are paid off.

Discretionary Income is income after subtracting taxes and your normal expenses such as rent or mortgage, utilities, insurance, medical, transportation, property maintenance, child support, inflation, food and other miscellaneous monthly expenses that you pay to maintain a certain standard of living that you desire.

• You now know that Disposable Income *differs from* Discretionary Income.

It is important that you distinguish in your mind that Disposable income is money that you have left after paying your taxes—while discretionary income is money you have left over after paying your taxes “and” mortgage/rent, food, utilities, and life's other necessities.

Disposable Income is income that you have at your disposal "after" the payment of taxes!

Discretionary Income is money that you can spend or save at your discretion after the payment of your taxes "and" monthly expenses!

You now know that disposable income and after-tax income are basically the same thing—just expressed differently.

• You now know that your Gross Income is your total personal income before taking taxes or deductions into account.

• You now know that your gross income is how much you make before taxes. Gross Income is the figure people are looking for when they ask you how much you gross a month.

• You now know that your Modified-Adjusted Gross Income varies according to purpose and who is requesting that you modify.

All modified versions may add certain items to AGI that were excluded in computing gross income.

Common additions include tax exempt interest and the excluded portion of Social Security benefits. Modified-Adjusted Gross Income (MAGI) is often used when calculating the alternative minimum tax (AMT).

You now know that your Net Income refers to take home pay, or the amount of money earned after payroll withholding such as state and federal income taxes, social security taxes, and pretax benefits like health insurance premiums.

In short, gross income less certain deductions equal Net Income.

• You now know that your Personal Income is basically your “Gross Income” that was discussed earlier. It is your total income before taxes or any deductions and can include various sources.

You know that your Personal Taxable Income is derived by including all taxable income sources and subtracting out adjustments, exclusions, deductions and credits—to determine your taxable income.

Make it a point to increase your income and reduce your expenses so that you can enhance the future for yourself and your family!

You already know that you can increase your income by making compound interest work for you and not against you?

By understanding and being able to distinguish among the various types of income and understanding how compounding works, you put yourself in position to understand your personal finances in a more intelligent (meaningful and effective way that works to your benefit) manner!

You also put yourself and your mind in a more favorable position where you can control your future in a more "financially alert manner" and in a manner that will lead to true and lasting success for you and your family!

And even though **inflation** is not income, it can negatively affect your income and your wealth building activities, therefore you want to be aware of the presence of inflation as the higher the inflation, the more your spending power will be affected in a negative way.

Inflation is normally present in all economic cycles, and you want to do your planning with the realization that inflation is real and can reduce your realized gains in the current economy—or any economy.

Understanding Your Net Worth

Although wealth building is a lofty goal, many have no clue or are totally unaware of where they now stand financially as it relates to their finances and particularly their net worth as they attempt to build wealth.

At this time you will learn how you can integrate your understanding of how you manage your finances on a daily basis with the knowledge that you need to know that can help you "increase your net worth" and ultimately your wealth, so that you can live in a manner that will bring you the joy that you desire on a continuous basis!

It is very important that you have a real understanding of what you own (your current assets) and what you owe (your current liabilities) as that is a critical factor as you move forward in your financial life. It is also very important that you at this time come to the full realization that your **"self-worth"** is far more important than your **"net worth"** as you build wealth!

In simple form, theory and practice you can determine your net worth by creating a personal balance sheet so that you will know what you own and what you owe (assets minus liabilities equal net worth) and create a level of comfort or discomfort within your mind–depending on the "outcome of the number that you come up with"–as it relates to your net worth at this time.

However, even if the number that you come up with is not to your liking, you can change all of that by making the decision to do so and then putting an action plan in place that will take you to where you need or desire to be.

If your net worth is not at an acceptable level, you can take real steps that can ensure that you will get your finances to an acceptable level or to the level that will make life more meaningful and enjoyable for you and your family!

If your net worth is at an acceptable level you can continue to make good decisions as it relates to your finances and build the type of wealth that will take you toward the net worth that you desire or toward the net worth that will make life "more enjoyable" for you and your family.

You can start on a journey of **improving your net worth** so that you can do what you really desire to do during your lifetime by taking several important steps:

It is in your best short and long term interest to know your net worth at the earliest point possible and to make plans to improve your net worth at the earliest time possible.

It is your responsibility to know where you stand financially and it is your responsibility to put in place a plan that will reduce or eliminate your debt so that you can start on a serious journey to building wealth and increasing your net worth.

Your sincere approach to eliminating debt, increasing your income and building wealth in a manner that truly serves your best interest is a major factor in helping you get on a fast track path to making life more enjoyable for you, your loved ones—and others as you navigate through life on planet earth.

Always remember that the more focused you are toward improving your net worth—the more mental energy you can pull up from inside your mind that can take you toward your goals more efficiently.

Be sure to put your goals in writing to help clarify your intent so that you can focus your resources (financial and non-financial) on things that really matter in your life. By doing so you will increase your net worth and build your wealth more efficiently over the coming years.

Calculate your net worth now by going to Kiplinger.com net worth page...

1) Know how to use personal financial statements to your advantage

If you approach your finances with the creation and understanding of a personal budget or cash flow statement, you can put yourself in position to make the right–or at a minimum a good decision(s) as it relates to your financial future.

You also need to create a personal income statement if you desire even more clarity about where you are headed as far as your finances are concerned. You can look at your personal income statement in the same manner as your cash flow statement, however it is on a 12-month or annual basis, whereas your cash flow statement or budget is on a monthly basis.

In addition, a personal balance sheet will provide you the knowledge of where you stand financially as far as your net worth is concerned.

The higher your net worth, the better off you are doing financially. You can purchase Managing & Improving Your Credit & Finances for this Millennium and learn about ways that you can attack your net worth before and after you retire in ways you may have never imagined.

You can go to Kiplinger.com, right now to see where you now stand as far as your net worth is concerned. Be sure you have accurate numbers as it relates to your assets and liabilities.

By doing so you can put yourself in better position to achieve the goals that you desire to attain during your lifetime.

2) Know how to manage your credit effectively throughout your lifetime

It is important that you skillfully manage your credit affairs and you don't let creditors skillfully manage you to the point where you operate from a disadvantage.

Why should you operate from a vantage point of disadvantage when you can have creditors operate from a point of disadvantage—if you gain and utilize the right knowledge?

By mastering what it takes to manage your credit effectively throughout your lifetime you put yourself in position to achieve at an optimal level throughout your lifetime and at the same time put yourself in position to use credit wisely or in a manner where you come out ahead!

3) Know all areas of your finances that you must address and then address those areas appropriately

By knowing and understanding your personal financial statements, knowing how to skillfully manage your credit and having a real understanding of where you want to take your future, you are now ready to look at your finances in a comprehensive manner and make moves based on that analysis that will help further increase your net worth as you build wealth.

By knowing all areas of your finances that you must address and acting in a positive way with that knowledge, you can put yourself in position to attain many of the goals that you may have thought about—but never thought you would achieve during your lifetime.

At this stage you would put together written plans that would lead you toward reaching your goals in a realistic manner.

Conclusion or Key Points

By understanding how compounding works, understanding the various types of income, using financial statements to your advantage by reviewing your current cash flow and making improvements where needed, cutting your expenses and getting more income (if you need to do so), you are getting on a real path toward "increasing your net worth" and the success that you desire is more likely to occur.

However, you can't stop there!

You must know what you own (your assets) and what you owe (your liabilities) so that you can readily determine your net worth.

Your goal on an annual basis is to always increase your net worth!

By having the appropriate insurance in all areas (including homeowners insurance), you help reduce your financial risks and your path toward increasing your net worth will be made in a more effortless manner!

Additionally by having a comprehensive or wholesome view of your finances you put yourself in position to reduce your stress levels and achieve your goals in a more effortless manner once you implement your plan for success on a consistent basis.

Chapter 7 Artificial Intelligence, Fraud & Wealth Building

Learn the importance of effectively using AI and your need to guard against fraud and the unwise use of credit...

Although **AI** (**A**rtificial **I**ntelligence) is a great time saver and can enhance your results in many endeavors, **AI** cannot substitute from you applying yourself and using your own intelligence **(RI or R**eal **I**ntelligence**)** to achieve more.

You want to utilize real intelligence that you have, along with artificial intelligence to build wealth more efficiently and help you improve on other tasks.

It is important that you **intelligently pursue your wealth building efforts** with what you "have within" so that you can reach the goals that you desire, avoid a financial quagmire, and pursue goals that are higher and not remain where you are–or worst yet fall short of reaching your goals and face consequences that are dire.

It is important that you come up with a real way that you can more intelligently pursue your goals–starting today!

1) Financial uncertainty by many is understandable in the current environment

Even though uncertainty about your future is expected at this time based on all that is happening, you must also expect success throughout your lifetime, despite the uncertainty that is in the air at this and any other time. At this time (fall 2025) the atmosphere around the world and particularly in the United States is at a level unseen by many during their lifetime, and for most the atmosphere does not exude positivity.

With tariffs, tax and spending bills that take away from the least who are in need and move advantages to millionaires and billionaires, the atmosphere is depressing for many.

Despite what is occurring, it is important that you recognize and realize what is outside of your control and what you control so that you can take steps to at a minimum improve your situation at this time and in the coming years–particularly with the uncertainty that is now in the environment.

2) Lack of action by you and others at this or any time is not acceptable if you desire more

The steps that you can take may not be visible to you at this time, however if you take action and sincerely want to learn and apply steps that can lead to you controlling your outcomes as opposed to having your outcomes directed by **AI** and other disadvantageous means–the solution for you is to take proactive action and control your own life proactively—not reactively–now that is **R**eal **I**ntelligence!

However, **AI** has its purpose as it can assist you on many tasks and assignments that you may have on a daily basis. Whether ChatGPT, Grok, Copilot, Deepseek, Grammarly, Gemini, DeepL or any others, you want to know the advantages and disadvantages while using them as they all have limitations.

For those who are business owners, **AI** has the potential to run all areas of your company, can help schedule your day, pull up demographic data in your area, and can craft a personality profile that caters to your type of business–among other abilities! **AI** combined with **RI** can greatly enhance your life and possibly give you a competitive advantage when used appropriately.

It is important that you realize that adversity or unwanted happenings will occur throughout your life and at varying degrees–and in many cases on multiple fronts, therefore you want to **equip your mind with all that you can** to better manage the adversity that you will undoubtedly face so that you can still achieve–even if you have to re-strategize along the way to achieve your goals.

3) You possess the ability to transform your current situation into that of lasting success

By possessing in your mind what you have learned, you are now in position to grow and pursue other areas of wealth building that you need to know. You want to be aware of what you need to do to more efficiently make your dreams come true–and although **AI** has many benefits, it is **R**eal **I**ntelligence that will better direct you toward making your dreams come true.

That is not to say that artificial intelligence **(AI)** should play no role, however you want to use **AI** and other tools effectively–therefore, you must be more aware of the limitations and potential of technology, as real success begins and ends inside of you!

Your awareness of the need to pursue your goals more aggressively at this time can help you transform your finances and position you to have the ability to do what you desire at the various stages of your life. However, it is important that you pursue your goals at your highest level as you possess in your heart and mind the knowledge (or will soon possess) that is necessary to do just that.

Your ability to believe in, educate, and use your own mind throughout your lifetime for the benefit of yourself and your family can lead to you not only pursuing more, but also achieving more–in large part because you made the commitment to open a new door.

Although an economy of uncertainty can occur at any time, you can use **R**eal **I**ntelligence to move forward with more confidence and optimism in spite of the current economy or any economy. The **AI** revolution, robots, humanoids, driverless vehicles, drone technology, smart homes, smart buildings, tariffs and the state of leadership worldwide, and particularly in the United States, all signal an uncertain future when looked at objectively. However, it is up to you to turn what appears to be a turbulent economy for an uncertain period into a successful period for you and your family.

You must open your own door if you sincerely desire to soar and using **R**eal **I**ntelligence that you possess in your heart and mind, can put you on a path to achieving the type of success that is one of a kind, and prior to you making a "real commitment" in your life, may have been hard to find.

Now is the time that you let joy in, have appreciation for being here, and show gratitude for what you have done ***and will do*** *so that your heart and mind is at peace, because you control not only* ***AI****, but also* ***RI****!*

That **r**eal **i**ntelligence includes analyzing your finances in 3 steps (or other ways that you may find effective) that you have learned throughout this book and making improvements as best you can on a continuous basis. Keep in mind that still requires planning for the long-term, if you are now in position to do so! It also means having backup plan(s) and the ability to pivot, when necessary, based on economic conditions.

Although chaos, confusion and lack of action by many is currently flowing in the atmosphere and have some in a state of anxiety, you want to operate internally with confidence and not act from a position of weakness–as you must move to action as if you are running in the Preakness (at a pace that is disciplined and uniquely your own).

Although **A**rtificial **I**ntelligence can play a major role in human advancement and possibly make many of your daily tasks less taxing, you want to know in definite terms that the **R**eal **I**ntelligence that you possess is far superior, and even in times of uncertainty you can live simply (with less stress) by knowing in clear terms what you need to do and will do, so that you can laugh more, **love more** and sincerely open a new door!

At the same time, you don't want to be afraid of **AI** as it has numerous roles, therefore you can use **AI** to perform many tasks for you throughout your lifetime. Even when it comes to building wealth, **AI** can help you evaluate potential investment returns in say, a target date fund, index fund, ETF fund and other mutual funds and recommend the best pick–for starters. Furthermore, you want to know that **AI** has really been around for decades and has really become prominent in the last few years.

Other major advancements in **AI** over the past few years include remote patient monitoring advancements, doctor visit preparation by patients asking the right questions and seeking the right answers prior to doctor visits, advanced accessibility options for those who don't hear or see well, along with major advancements in how entertainment can enter your life–along with countless other capabilities.

Even with advancements, many **AI platforms** are notorious for providing unreliable information, therefore it is your responsibility to decipher the quality of the information/answers using **RI**, along with doing additional research and/or talking with professionals and others who may have more knowledge of the subject matter than you.

However, the key to success using **AI** and **RI** is to control **AI** and not let **AI** control you by asking the right question(s) and seeking the right answers (in all facets of your life)–and always realize the limitations while using! By doing so you are showing **R**eal **I**ntelligence and the success that you desire will be out in front of you and will be yours to GRAB! You also want to be aware of those who use **AI** against you to your detriment–as that can prevent you from making your dreams come true.

Always realize and be cognizant that **AI is only as good as the input that is utilized**–therefore always keep that in mind as there can be bias and incorrect data outputs when that occurs!

All the best to your **real success,** as you deserve "nothing that is artificial" as you build wealth, due in large part because you are "willing to apply" your **R**eal **I**ntelligence and give it your absolute best while others rest.

Fraud, Credit Management & Wealth Building

It is important that you are aware of fraud prevention actions that you can make proactively as well as ways that you can avoid the unwise use of credit.

As you build wealth in the current economy you want to know that even with technology improvements, data breaches occur on a consistent basis, therefore you want to know how to **guard against the breaching of your data** and do all you can on the front end to prevent data breaches. Even in the unfortunate times when data breaches occur, you want to be in position to respond more effectively in the event of a data breach that involves "your" identifying information.

You also want to be aware of credit and finance promotional offers that you may be bombarded with at the various stages of your life as many offer credit to unsuspecting consumers at high rates of interest or terms and conditions that work for their (credit issuer's) best interest–and not yours.

And just as you must be aware of how you build wealth from an internal point of view, you also need to be aware of fraudsters and scammers who are all around you (external or outside point of view), if you sincerely desire to achieve at a higher level than most.

As you build wealth, it is important that you **guard against fraud in various forms** and you must be more aware of unscrupulous creditors and others who are working day and night to entice you into making decisions that "are not good" for you and your family.

Be particularly aware of bank imposters who claim there is an issue with your account who want you to withdraw or move money, those who offer false ticket sales on websites and social media and those who offer "get rich quick" investment scams on websites or over social media.

By utilizing credit monitoring, freezing of your credit and fraud alerts–you can better protect your finances and achieve more throughout your lifetime. And even though it may cost you time at the front-end, it will help you avoid or reduce your heartache at the back-end!

Credit monitoring allows you to review the accounts on your credit reports from one or more of the 3 national credit reporting agencies. You can go to annualcreditreport.com (877-322-8228) to get a free report from each bureau once per year or you can purchase a copy.

Keep in mind that bank accounts and payday loans that could be opened using your identifying information would not be picked up by most monitoring services.

*Whether you utilize free sites or paid sites–in this day and time you want to **monitor** your accounts, either by self-monitoring or a paid service:*

Transunion

PO Box 1000

Chester, PA 19016-1000

1-800-888-4213

www.transunion.com

Equifax

PO Box 740241

Atlanta, GA 30374-0241

1-866-349-5191

www.equifax.com

Experian

PO Box 2002

Allen, TX 75013-9701

1-866-200-6020

www.experian.com

Freezing your credit allows you to freeze your credit file so that no new credit can be opened in your name "without" the use of a **PIN or (Personal Identification Number)** that is issued to you when you initiate a freeze.

The goal of freezing your credit is to prevent potential credit grantors from accessing your credit report without your consent.

You must temporarily lift the freeze for creditors to gain access. You will in essence have a "delay" in your ability to obtain credit. If you were looking to buy a house and get a home mortgage–there would be a delay but generally not be of consequence. By law credit freezes are available at no cost to you, however **you must contact each credit bureau individually** to implement the freeze.

Lifting of Freeze–online or by phone the credit reporting agency must do so within **1 hour**–by mail 3 business days.

Implementing a freeze–online or by phone the credit reporting agency has **1 business day** after receiving your request–by mail 3 business days.

NOTE: The IRS also offers an **I**dentity **P**rotection **PIN** or **IP PIN** that you can utilize to help safeguard against the fraudulent filing of your taxes.

If you are now or in the future the victim of a data breach you may want to consider ***freezing*** *your credit and/or getting an IP PIN (IRS.gov):*

Transunion

PO Box 160

Woodlyn, PA 19094

1-800-916-8800

www.transunion.com/credit-freeze

Equifax

PO Box 105788

Atlanta, GA 30348-5788

1-888-298-0045

www.equifax.com/personal/credit-report-services

Experian

PO Box 9554

Allen, TX 75013-9554

1-888-397-3742

www.experian.com/freeze/center.html

Fraud alerts will allow you to place an "initial" or "extended" fraud alert on your file(s) at no cost.

Upon seeing a fraud alert a business is required to take steps to verify your identity "before" extending new credit. **If you are a victim of ID theft you can extend the alert for up to 7 years!** By contacting one bureau and placing the alert–they will notify the other 2 bureaus.

*You also have the option to put an initial **fraud alert** on your account that is valid for one year if you desire additional protection on top of monitoring and freezing of your credit:*

Transunion

PO Box 2000

Chester, PA 19016-2000

1-800-680-7289

www.transunion.com/fraud-alerts

Equifax

PO Box 105069

Atlanta, GA 30348-5069

1-800-525-6285

www.equifax.com/personal/credit-report-services/credit-fraud-alerts/

Experian

PO Box 9554

Allen, TX 75013-9554

1-888-397-3742

www.experian.com/fraud/center.html

By utilizing credit monitoring, freezing of your credit and fraud alerts–you can better protect your finances and achieve more in a safer way. They are cost effective ways that you can use to prevent, respond to, or minimize the effects of fraud in your life.

Although setting up fraud alerts and freezing your credit will take time, it will be worth every minute if you can prevent unauthorized activity on your financial accounts.

Credit monitoring ***(make sure all 3 credit bureaus are being monitored with the service you select)*** *will also take a few minutes a week of your time and it too can be time that is well spent.*

You can now set up credit alerts and other alerts with your creditors, bankers and others whom you have a financial relationship with that will provide alerts and monitor your information on the world wide web, including the dark web.

Other Options:

Contact the FTC and Your State AG's Office

If you find information on your credit report that appears fraudulent or you feel information on you have been misused, you can also contact your local law enforcement and the **FTC** and your states **A**ttorney **G**eneral'**s** office. Be sure to get a copy of the police report as the report can potentially relieve you of the debt obligation created by the fraudster with your creditor(s).

Federal **T**rade **C**ommission

FTC Consumer Response Center

600 Pennsylvania Avenue, NW

Washington, DC 20580

1-877-IDTHEFT (438-4338)

www.ftc.gov/bcp/edu/microsites/idtheft

The above contact data for the 3 credit bureaus and the FTC are current as of 10/14/2025

If you suspect Investment Fraud:

Call—**800-732-0330** SEC Commission or go to www.sec.gov

To obtain background information on a broker or brokerage firm call **800-289-9999** or go to www.finra.org/investors/toolscalculator/brokercheck

On your **personal taxes** you can help prevent fraud by getting an **IP PIN** that will help prevent the fraudulent filing of taxes by a fraudster as they will need to know your PIN even if they have your other identifying data.

You can utilize this approach annually and receive a new IP PIN annually from the IRS.

Credit Solicitations, Fraud & Wealth Building

In the current economy credit offers abound, and if you are new to credit or lack the needed credit management skills, you can find yourself victim to unscrupulous creditors.

It is not uncommon for college graduates, undergraduates, the elderly, those new to the job market and others to receive offers from various creditors, and many jump at those offers with no real concern for their future obligations (they fail to begin with the end in mind). Many creditors offer to loan you money or provide actual checks that you can cash immediately that are tempting and could put you on the hook of paying interest at rates over 30%.

Other offers may appear more reasonable such as 8% or less, however they too can put you in a more dire position if you jump at the offer and you do not have a comprehensive overview of your finances. Still others will offer you credit cards of varying credit limits–even if you have no need or desire to utilize credit or have a credit file.

You want to look at the fine print of all offers that you are considering and know the details of your engagement on the front end–not after the fact.

Does your acceptance of credit offer line up with your goals and do you have mastery over credit so that credit issuers don't have mastery over ***(they know you don't know what you need to know)*** *you, because you lack mastery over credit?*

You want to know your **APR**, **Finance Charge**, **Amount Financed** and your **Total Payments** prior to engagement with creditors, as by knowing that information you can determine how bad (or good) the offer really is. You also want to have mastery over the "5 Credit Factors" so you can avoid the unwise use of credit and put yourself in a deeper financial hole.

In many instances **you have better options,** and you want to pursue those options "prior to" making a bad decision or a decision that you will later regret due to lack of preparation, high pressure, lack of knowledge, time limit pressure and other negative occurrences whether created by you or outside forces!

You want to guard against **identity theft** and other **occurrences or potential occurrences of a negative nature** in your credit and financial life.

Even the federal government in the United States are taking steps to reduce fraud as they now (2024 and beyond) require many small employers that are LLC's or Corporations to provide certain **(BOIR) b**eneficial **o**wnership **i**nformation **r**eporting, so that illicit pass-through activity and reporting can be better traced. This report is required by FinCen and the deadline for reporting was January 1, 2025, however there have been delays.

Phone and email fraudsters are out in abundance and their goal is to get you to provide personally identifiable data or get you to click on dangerous links whether text or email. Other fraudsters and scammers will attempt to gain your trust and get you to provide usernames and passwords so that they can access your data and ultimately breach your accounts.

If you desire a more comprehensive approach in the management and protection of your credit and finances, consider purchasing **1-2-3 Credit & Me** and take life changing control of your finances from this day forward in a way that can put you on a path to achieving all of your goals in a more definitive way.

You already know the importance of "looking within yourself" and improving in areas that you are weak in.

You also need to look at the external environment (political, regulatory, economic, societal, technological and legal happenings where you reside) to see moves that you can potentially make that will serve your better interests in the short and long-term. In the societal realm, you may have unscrupulous players who may be out to scam you out of your hard-earned cash.

In the event that your data is breached and your identifying information is under the care of a company or industry, many will notify you of the breach and often provide free credit monitoring for a year or more if you sign up–and if you find yourself a victim and the service is offered, you want to strongly consider it, particularly if you do not have a paid service at the time of the breach.

If you are elderly, you want to be particularly cautious about financial moves that you anticipate making!

You don't have to put yourself in position to be taken advantage of by creditors, lenders, scammers and others–as you deserve a better approach when it comes to the management of your credit and finances, and **you now have those approaches at your fingertips**, if you are now ready to take action of a proactive nature!

To help prevent fraud, you want to implement common sense actions that you can take yourself to prevent scams such as:

*Filter unwanted emails to your spam folder and block unwanted calls and texts and do updates and use the latest internet search browser when possible!

*Don't give in to anyone pressuring or threatening you into giving them your personal information!

*Hang up phone or don't respond to requests for information or money on contacts (calls, emails, text messages etcetera) that you did not initiate!

*Even if you are contacted by a business that you recognize, don't give out your personal or financial info to anyone!

*If anyone says you must act immediately, stop and ask–is this how a company that I wish to do business with should act? If you feel uneasy, there is a good chance that you are right!

*Instead of clicking links in emails and text messages or calling numbers that you did not request, use a company's real contact information from their "official" website!

*If someone tells you to keep a secret or say something suspicious and you are not comfortable, stop the conversation and discuss what has occurred with a trusted family member or someone else you trust!

*Be sure to consider multi-factor authentication with your banking, investment, retirement and other financial accounts–particularly those with large balances or high credit limits!

*Be on the lookout for those who pretend to be someone you know, offer you a prize or the ability to help you or a family member get out of trouble, pressure you to act before you have had time to think it over, and ask you to pay in a specific manner whether by payment app, wire, gift card or check!

You want to **remain vigilant and be alert for incidents of fraud** by reviewing account statements and monitoring free or paid credit reports that are available. Look for accounts or creditor inquiries that you did not initiate or recognize and make sure all your data in your credit files from all three credit reporting agencies are accurate.

Also be alert for suspicious calls and emails and never give out identifying information unless you initiate the call or email, and you are certain of who you are communicating with!

Always realize that you have rights under the **fair credit reporting act (FCRA)** which governs the collection and use of information about you by consumer reporting agencies. You can learn more about your rights under the **FCRA** by going to:

www.consumer.ftc.gov/sites/default/files/articles/pdf/pdf-0096-fair-credit-reporting-act.pdf

In addition to being alert for fraudsters and scammers, you also want to be aware of marketing activity that may be aimed at you that promotes reward and other credit cards, retail cards, personal loans and other promotions of varying types as they can in many cases lead you astray–and off of your well planned path that you need or plan to take.

You want to determine as best you can on the front end if the promotion that is offered fits in with your goals–whether they be your short, intermediate, or long-term goals.

Generally, if you have 5 or 6 credit cards that would possibly be sufficient for building and maintaining your credit as long as you are managing them effectively over time on a **consistent basis**—ultimately it all depends on your goals. If you have credit card debt and desire to pay the debt off efficiently with lower interest going to the credit issuer, let's say you have credit card debt of $4,000 and you get a zero percent promotion offer and you generally know that you can qualify based on your credit score–you still want to run the numbers upfront to determine if there is a real benefit for you.

Can I pay off the $4,000 with the discretionary income that I have available in the 18 month zero percent interest payment promotional period or window and still meet all of my other obligations on a monthly basis?

To eliminate the debt of $4,000 you would have to pay roughly $220 per month for the next 18 months!

In addition, if you apply for a new card you generally won't know the credit amount that you would be approved for in advance and you would normally have a 3% or 4% transfer fee, meaning if you were to transfer $4,000 of debt, your new balance with the credit issuer would be $4,120 at a 3% transfer rate or $4,160 at a 4% transfer rate.

If you were paying interest monthly at 20% on a $4,000 balance prior to the transfer, your monthly interest would be roughly $80 per month–meaning in 2 or 3 months **you would have paid more than the transfer fee**–giving you a real opportunity to pay off your remaining balance in roughly 18 months at zero percent interest–saving you well over $1,000 whether the transfer fee was 3% or 4%–therefore **there is a serious advantage for you to transfer in this scenario** if you have the "discretionary income" and credit score that qualifies you for the promotional credit card with a credit limit of $4,000 or higher–and even less–depending on your goals!

You also must be disciplined and highly motivated to pay off the debt in an efficient manner!

Once that payoff of $4,000 has ended after 18 months, you could choose to invest that $220 that you have become accustomed to living without for say–10, 20, or 30 years and have a nice windfall in a relatively painless way!

It is important that you always realize that unscrupulous actors are all around you and particularly as it relates to your finances and the building of wealth, however there is no reason for you to fear your financial future if you get out in front of your finances. It is your responsibility to put yourself in a winning financial position so that you can't be easily taken advantage of as it relates to your finances!

By understanding the life stages of your financial life and **looking at your finances in a comprehensive way** at the earliest time possible, you can put yourself in position for greater success and better guard against fraudulent actors that will eventually come your way at some point in your life.

You also want to be aware of the IRS "Dirty Dozen" Scams that are now prevalent.

Many schemes are year-round and threaten your annual tax return. The scams are evolving and changing from year to year. For 2025 they include:

1) **Email phishing scams:** The IRS continues to see a barrage of email and text scams targeting taxpayers and others. Taxpayers and tax professionals should be alert to fake communications from entities posing as legitimate organizations in the tax and financial community, including the IRS, state tax agencies and tax software companies. These messages arrive in the form of unsolicited texts or emails to lure unsuspecting victims into providing valuable personal and financial information that can lead to identity theft.

There are two main types:

- **Phishing:** An email sent by fraudsters claiming to come from the IRS. The email lures the victims into the scam with a variety of ruses such as enticing victims with a phony tax refund or threatening them with false legal or criminal charges for tax fraud.
- **Smishing:** A text or smartphone SMS message where scammers often use alarming language such as, "Your account has now been put on hold," or "Unusual Activity Report," with a bogus "Solutions" link to restore the recipient's account. The promise of unexpected tax refunds is another potential tactic used by scam artists.

As a reminder, never click on any unsolicited communication claiming to be from the IRS as it may surreptitiously load malware. This may also be a way for malicious hackers to load ransomware that keeps the legitimate user from accessing their system and files.

The IRS has special information available to help people understand and report email scams.

2) **Bad social media advice:** Another growing concern in 2025 continues to involve incorrect tax information on social media that can mislead honest taxpayers with bad advice, potentially leading to identity theft and tax problems. Social media platforms routinely circulate inaccurate or misleading tax information, including TikTok where people share wildly inaccurate tax advice. Some involve urging people to misuse common tax documents like Form W-2.

The IRS and CASST warn people not to fall for these scams, and urge them to follow trusted social media advice from the IRS, tax professionals and other reputable sources. The IRS reminds taxpayers who knowingly file fraudulent tax returns that they could potentially face significant civil and criminal penalties.

3) **IRS Individual Online Account help from scammers:** Swindlers can pose as a "helpful" third party and offer to help create a taxpayer's IRS Individual Online Account at IRS.gov. In reality, no help is needed, and the agency offers tips on how to sign up and avoid scams. The IRS Individual Online Account provides taxpayers with valuable personal tax information. But watch out: Third parties making these offers will try to steal a taxpayer's personal information and try to submit fraudulent tax returns in the victim's name to get a big refund.
4) **Fake charities:** Bogus charities are a perennial problem that can intensify whenever a crisis or natural disaster strikes. Scammers set up these fake organizations to take advantage of the public's generosity.

They seek money and personal information, which can be used to further exploit victims through identity theft.

Taxpayers who give money or goods to a charity might be able to claim a deduction on their federal tax return if they itemize deductions, but charitable donations only count if they go to a qualified tax-exempt organization recognized by the IRS.

5) **False Fuel Tax Credit claims:** A major concern during the past year involved taxpayers who were misled into believing they were eligible for the Fuel Tax Credit. The credit is meant for off-highway business and farming use and is not available to most taxpayers. However, unscrupulous tax return preparers and promoters, including people on social media, continue enticing taxpayers into inflating their refunds by erroneously claiming the credit. The IRS has seen an increase in the promotion of filing certain refundable credits using Form 4136, Credit for Federal Tax Paid on Fuels. The IRS urges people to get more information and ensure they are properly claiming this credit.
6) **Credits for Sick Leave and Family Leave:** This specialized credit is available for self-employed individuals for 2020 and 2021 during the pandemic; the credit is not available for later tax years. The IRS is seeing repeated instances where taxpayers are using Form 7202, Credits for Sick Leave and Family Leave for Certain Self-Employed Individuals, to incorrectly claim a credit based on income earned as an employee and not as a self-employed individual.
7) **Bogus self-employment tax credit:** Social media advice continues to circulate about a non-existent "Self-Employment Tax Credit" that's misleading taxpayers into filing false claims. Promoters market it as a way for self-employed people and gig workers to get big payments for the COVID-19 pandemic period. Like misleading marketing around the Employee Retention Credit, there is inaccurate

information being circulated that suggests many people qualify for the tax credit and payments of up to $32,000 when they do not.

The underlying credit being referred to in social media is not called the "Self-Employment Tax Credit," it's a much more limited and technical credit called the Credits for Sick Leave and Family Leave. Many people simply do not qualify for these credits, and the IRS is closely reviewing claims coming in under this provision, so taxpayers filing claims do so at their own risk.

8) **Improper household employment taxes:** Taxpayers "invent" fictional household employees and then file Schedule H (Form 1040), Household Employment Taxes, to claim a refund based on false sick and family medical leave wages they never paid.
9) **The overstated withholding scam:** This is a recent scheme circulating on social media encouraging people to fill out Form W-2, Wage and Tax Statement, or other forms like Form 1099-NEC and other 1099s with false income and withholding information.

In this overstated withholding scheme, scam artists suggest people make up large income and withholding amounts as well as the fictional employer supplying those amounts. Scam artists then instruct people to file the bogus tax return electronically in hopes of getting a substantial refund due to the large amount of fraudulent withholding.

If the IRS cannot verify the wages, income or withholding credits entered on the tax return, the tax refund will be held pending further review. Taxpayers should always file a complete and accurate tax return. They should only use legitimate information returns, such as an employer issued Form W-2, to complete returns correctly.

There are multiple variations of the overstated withholding credit scheme, including those involving Forms W-2 and W-2G; Forms 1099-R, 1099-NEC, 1099-DIV, 1099-OID and 1099-B; as well as the Alaskan Dividend Fund, Schedule K-1 with Withholding Reported, and Unspecified Source of Withholding Credit Claimed.

10) **Misleading Offers in Compromise:** The Offers in Compromise (OIC) program is an important program that helps people settle their federal tax debts when they are unable to pay in full. But "mills" can aggressively promote Offers in Compromise in misleading ways to people who clearly don't meet the qualifications, frequently costing taxpayers thousands of dollars. A taxpayer can check their eligibility for free using the IRS Offer in Compromise Pre-Qualifier tool.

11) **Ghost tax return preparers:** Most tax preparers provide outstanding professional service. However, people should be careful of shady tax professionals and watch for common warning signs, including charging a fee based on the size of the refund. A major red flag or bad sign is when the tax preparer is unwilling to sign the return. Avoid these "ghost" preparers, who will prepare a tax return but refuse to sign or include their IRS Preparer Tax Identification Number (PTIN) as required by law. Taxpayers should never sign a blank or incomplete return. Instead, the IRS reminds taxpayers to turn to a trusted tax professional for help.

12) **New client scams and spear phishing:** In 2025, the IRS continues to see the "new client" scam, which involves spear phishing attempts that target tax pros. Cybercriminals impersonate new, potential clients to trick tax professionals and other businesses into responding to their emails. Once the tax pro responds, the scammer sends a malicious attachment or URL that can compromise the preparer's computer systems and allow the attacker to access sensitive client information.

Phishing is a term given to emails or text messages designed to get users to provide personal information, and spear phishing is a phishing attempt tailored to a specific organization or business. Tax professionals frequently find themselves a target of this type of scam.

Spear phishing holds greater potential for harm because a successful spear phishing attack can ultimately steal client data and the tax pro's identity, allowing the thief to file fraudulent returns using the stolen information.

Businesses and individuals, including tax pros, should always be cautious and look out for any suspicious requests or unusual behavior before sharing any sensitive information or responding to an email.

Warning signs include poorly constructed sentences and unusual word choices. Be aware that by gaining access to a hacked email account, scammers can locate a genuine email from a previous victim's email account sent to their tax professional.

All the best to using AI to your advantage, avoiding fraud, avoiding being susceptible to non-beneficial marketing techniques, avoiding the unwise use of credit and otherwise turning your finances into a mess.

Conclusion or Key Points

You want to be aware at the earliest point possible of how **AI** is spreading and prepare for the changes that are underway. You also want to avoid becoming a victim of fraud in all its various and unscrupulous forms and avoid being manipulated by varying marketing techniques that work against your best interest.

In reality as you pursue your goals, there may be setbacks along the way and that is why you must also properly establish an emergency fund if you have not already done so.

In addition, you must manage your credit optimally and not let your credit manage you (pull you in directions that are not of "your" choosing). You must further look at ways that you can manage your insurance, investments, taxes, education funding, estate planning/wills and retirement planning in a way that will take you toward your goals in a more effective and efficient manner.

Additionally, you must not be intimidated by **A**rtificial **I**ntelligence as it has played a negative role in the consumer confidence of many and will continue to evolve. You want to position yourself to be able to take advantage of the advantages of **AI** (pun intended) and be wary and on alert for the disadvantages that can work against your best interests

All the best to your new level of success...

Chapter 8 Output & Wealth Building

Learn the importance of increasing your output as you build wealth...

During various economic cycles many feel drained by all that is happening, and many are apprehensive and/or uncertain about their future and how they can achieve more.

In this chapter you will learn ways that you can "increase your output" and achieve more in the current and future economic environments so that you can enjoy life on your terms.

As we all age here on planet earth the need for increased growth, and particularly financial growth for many is sorely needed at this time and this chapter will hopefully spark something on the inside of you to make you more aggressively pursue what you need to do regardless of your age–so that you can really make your dreams come true!

Increasing your output, at this time is what you need to do so that you can approach your finances in a better way, and it is a topic that is very important as you pursue your goals from day to day! Furthermore an "increase in output" is what is needed at this time based on the state of the economy in many areas; therefore, it is the topic of this chapter and hopefully will inspire and lead you and others toward achieving more throughout your lifetime!

It is important that you realize at the earliest time possible that you possess the ability to direct your future and achieve the outcomes that you desire, if you are willing to put forth the needed effort and reach higher!

In the paragraphs below you will learn **3 steps that you can take right now** that can put you on a path to **increasing your output** and achieving more at the various stages of your life.

1. In order to increase your output financially and build wealth more efficiently you must first determine where you are now at, and where you desire to go!

Your first step to achieving more and increasing your financial score is to **do an analysis of your cash flow** on a monthly and/or annual basis. By determining whether you have a monthly or annual surplus or deficit, you will know what you can potentially do to achieve more. Furthermore, you want to know what your assets and liabilities are so that you can determine your net worth and make plans for improving and increasing your net worth!

2. In order to increase your output, you must obtain "effective knowledge of your credit" so that you can achieve the goals that you desire throughout your lifetime. By doing so you can gain mastery of your credit so that you can make credit work for you as opposed to against you!

Your desire to understand and **master the 5 credit factors** can play an important role in your credit and financial management–and if you make a serious commitment at this time, you can put yourself in position to manage your credit effectively for the rest of your life, and eventually with less effort once you master what you need to know.

3. In order to increase your output you must manage your finances effectively and have the determination to achieve more! You must know what your finances consist of, and have a desire to improve upon and manage your finances in a wholesome manner so that you can achieve more!

Your desire to **increase your output** throughout your lifetime should provide you the motivation to learn and know that you must **more effectively manage your insurance, investments, taxes, emergency fund, education planning, estate planning/wills and retirement planning** in a way and manner that serves your and your family's best interest–not creditors or others who have no real concern for your financial future or outcomes that favor you and your family.

You must realize that you have the ability, capability, agility and capacity to do much more not only at this time, but at all times. Even when you face adversity, whether that adversity is brought to you or you find yourself in a position where you don't know what to do because you were the cause–you can still take the right actions that can **increase your output** and allow you to achieve your goals–after you take a short pause.

As you take steps to **increase your output,** you want to be awake so that you can take the right steps and make what you want to see occur–happen, as your goal is not to make a mistake. Isn't it time that you partake in your path to your own success for your own sake, and not achieve fleeting success that is fake?

Always realize that to increase your output you must operate with confidence and have clarity, or a clear vision of the success that you will soon achieve—or another way of looking at it–you must **sincerely** believe!

You also want to operate from this day forward with a high level of character and **not do like those** who operate in a "less than desirable manner" as they make a living and move along throughout their life!

Furthermore, your goal should be to live with joy at your center, have a real appreciation for your life, and have gratitude for what you have done and will do as you must change your attitude in order to reach your highest altitude!

You are now equipped to do far more than you are currently doing on a daily basis, and it is the desire of **The Art of Essential Action,** that you hit a grand slam as you round the bases and learn more about personal finance in new spaces.

Hopefully this chapter has given you meaningful direction so that you can **increase your output** and achieve more throughout your lifetime.

You want to give it your best so you can avoid a financial mess, journey toward success, **increase your output** and achieve at a level that is your absolute best.

You want to timely plant your seed (gain a solid financial foundation) in fertile soil so that you can have a bountiful harvest (achieve your financial and life goals) and enjoy life more.

With the changing of seasons around the world "sowing the ground" to bring in a bountiful harvest in due time is the goal of many.

In light of that fact, the topic of **reaping what you sow** is an appropriate topic to focus on in the remainder of this chapter as the concept can metaphorically play a role in improving your finances and building wealth during varying seasons.

Just as those who plant various fruits and vegetables in fertile soil and work the land–so too must you gain a **solid foundation** and **work toward reaching the goals that you desire** or the goals that you need to attain. You must not let unpredictable weather patterns (adversity) negatively affect your output as that should be expected if you are **sincere** about reaching your goals.

By planting **thoughts of success in your heart and mind** (planting seed in fertile soil) and putting together a plan that can get you the results that you desire, you can have a bountiful harvest (reach your financial goals) if you take the right action on a consistent basis along the way.

You must prepare your mind for the financial success that you desire, and you must have the mindset that you will reach higher.

You must create a personal cash flow statement to see where you now stand financially. It is akin to taking a soil sample to see what you are working with as far as the fertility of the ground is concerned. You want to ask yourself several key questions along the way, including:

- Do I have a "meaningful understanding" of personal financial statements?

    - Am I operating in good soil (visualizing clearly how I handle my income and expenses on a monthly basis) or do I need to amend the soil so that I can have a more bountiful harvest (move closer toward reaching my goals by getting more income, cutting expenses or doing a combination of the two) by having the discretionary income on a monthly basis that I desire to make life more enjoyable and meaningful for myself and my family?

- Do I fully understand the **"factors"** that affect my credit scores—including the ratios?

By understanding the factors that affect your credit, you are in effect helping to control the weather patterns (so you can sit out in the sun) as opposed to having the weather patterns control you (running you inside your house due to inclement weather).

You must know how a **P**ositive payment history, how you **U**tilize your credit, the **T**ime length of your credit, the **T**ype of credit that you have and **I**nquiries affect your credit and ultimately your financial future.

- Do I know all areas of my finances that I "must" address?

By planting in fertile soil, you will begin to see your harvest blossom in ways you never imagined. Also, by seeing your finances in a comprehensive way–you can achieve goals that you may have never thought possible.

You must have the knowledge to address your insurance, investments, taxes, emergency fund, education planning, estate planning/wills and retirement planning in as effective a manner as possible if you desire to achieve more during your lifetime.

In the times that are upon us currently, it is important that you look within and see how you operate when it comes to building wealth.

It is important that you put "your approach" to building wealth under a microscope to see if you can find ways to build wealth in a better, more effective, and more time efficient manner so that you can do more of what you and your family enjoy doing at this time and throughout your lifetime.

Your "enthusiasm to act effectively toward making what you desire to create or make happen in your life as it relates to the building of wealth" that allows you to live out your life with dignity can be made easier over the long-term if you pause now and look within to see ways that you can possibly do things better or more efficiently throughout your lifetime.

1) Do you even have an approach as it relates to the building of wealth?

Unlike many who live daily in free economy societies (knock on wood), and live daily in an aimless manner, you have an opportunity to have an approach to building wealth that is more certain, if you are now in the unfortunate position of not having an approach–or having a weak approach.

It is important that you use your self-awareness to determine if you have an effective approach to building wealth–or are you in need of an upgrade so that you can utilize a better path toward enduring success.

2) Do you know steps that you can take to begin to make things happen in your financial life?

There are many financial sources available that can direct you toward the steps that you can take to help you achieve more, and it is your responsibility to find those steps and utilize those steps to achieve more if you feel that those steps are for you!

You already know that it is your responsibility to know if your cash flow is positive or negative on a monthly and annual basis, along with knowing your balance sheet and net worth, so that you can achieve more throughout your lifetime.

3) Do you know the importance of your need to review to sincerely make your dreams come true?

As effective as you may think you are operating at this time with your current wealth building system (if you currently have one), you want to understand that with any system–you may fall short whether it be with your credit payoff plans or managing your finances in other areas, therefore you want to make adjustments when necessary and review on occasion to help ensure that you reach your goals in spite of setbacks that are seen in advance or even unseen with no warning.

You also want to have a "sincere approach" when you are building wealth, and you want to know the importance of reviewing to see if it provides you an avenue toward success that allows you to get to your destination efficiently. You must do this analysis in a clear, careful, analytical, accurate and critical manner if you desire to achieve at your highest level.

Your decision to look within and determine how you approach your wealth building efforts is a critical component of you achieving success in the short, intermediate, and long-term, and you want to do the needed analysis of your approach in a careful, critical and accurate manner. And by being **more aware** of how you operate within and without "proactively"–if you are one who sincerely desire to achieve more (pun intended), you can start or continue on a serious path toward improving your achievement score!

You must make it a priority to gain the mental fortitude to search out the best approaches that will take you toward the wealth building success that you need or deserve to achieve at the various stages of your life.

You must be excited and pursue your goals with more vigor so that you can avoid many of the common mistakes that many consumers make, have an understanding of your money management personality, know upfront that it will take effort to build wealth as nothing of real value will be given to you if you don't **put into action** what you need to do to make your dreams come true.

Always realize that fatigue and adversity will kick in at times, but you must continue to move forward and have a mindset that is unstoppable!

If you sincerely desire to build wealth, you will avoid intellectual laziness, and you will define your wealth building activities by courage and not cowardice–because you know the time is now for more action and less talk. Your pursuit of wealth building success must be more than just symbolic or performative towards your goals, your pursuit must be of substance!

Even though trade wars and social/economic growth are not congruent for growth in the larger economy generally in most countries, you want to eagerly pursue success in your personal economy specifically–at this time and throughout your lifetime.

In a nutshell, in order to achieve the results that you desire, you must act enthusiastically if you desire meaningful change in the current economy–or any economy!

Your "enthusiasm" or "passion" to manage your finances optimally throughout your lifetime and even after you transition, puts you on the right path toward success. By analyzing your wealth building approach under a microscope–you are now in position to do more than just hope.

You can now "use pro-action and not subtraction" to move forward because you are determined to put into action the required number of reps, as you are now "fully aware" of your required steps!

All the best to your timely wealth building success, due in large part because you decided to put procrastination to rest and increase your output and sincerely achieve success.

Conclusion or Key Points

When it comes to your finances you must know where you are now at and where you are going! You must encourage and inspire your loved ones and others to reach higher levels as well. Always know that at all times, you have the power to change the trajectory of your financial future!

Your application of what you have learned in this chapter must be balanced with the future goals that you desire or need to achieve.

It is important that you realize that what you **"learn, know, and apply"** empowers you to take more effective action as it relates to reaching your goals. You can make your road to success easier by applying the right principles at the right time during your life.

You can achieve many of your financial goals that may look impossible to achieve at this time if you pause and **put together an effective plan** that will take you to where you need or desire to be.

It is imperative that you leave your baggage (weeds) that is holding you back behind and turn something old into something new and better! Do something fresh today, respond to adversity in a strong fashion on a consistent basis as you now know a better way!

Why you must do what needs to be done now–without procrastination...

You can prevent the weeds from growing (avoid making mistakes) so that you won't have to repair the soil (waste valuable time and money when you could have avoided it).

You must realize that you must challenge yourself to do **far more than you are doing** at this time!

You must stick to it and move your PEN so you can WIN!

Let something original (a new rain cloud followed by unlimited sunshine) work its way into your life. Equip your mind for lasting success by gaining the skills that are needed to reach your future goals and use a comprehensive approach to manage your finances.

By doing so you are helping to ensure that you are equipped with the continuous financial success that you desire and deserve.

Be sure to apply what you learn in your everyday life. Your goal must be to be–and to do—not just know what to do and let what you know sit idly in your mind.

Your knowledge of the above material alone is not enough—action is what really counts.

Just as a farmer can't just throw out seeds and hope for the best, so too can't you, as someone who sincerely desire wealth building success, just think about a successful future and hope for the best!

NOW is the time that you plan appropriately, do what you need to do at the time that is right for you, and review in the best manner possible based on the **seeds** that are in your possession so that you can truly grow and put yourself and your family in the know!

By sowing your seed in a **fertile environment** you are helping to ensure that you do all that you need to do and more as you move toward your financial goals. You are helping your financial growth process and at the same time ensuring that a **bountiful harvest** is in your and your family's future.

You are on a real path to **reaping what you sow** because you have taken the time to gain the preparation and knowledge that can make your future glow–and more importantly you are learning what you need to put yourself in the know–and taking real steps on a path to obtaining financial results that will show!

You are on a path toward attaining a Financially Alert Mind (as opposed to just Financial Literacy) that will allow you to weather the elements as you reach toward your goals throughout your lifetime.

Always remember that you will be known not only for the impact that you have in your own life, but also the impact that you have on others. By effectively applying what you are learning, you can have a positive impact on others and reach the goals that you desire as well!

It is the goal of "The Art of Essential Action" that you are now in better position to "Sow the Financial Future" that "you" desire and receive a "Bountiful Harvest" in your due season.

Isn't the time right for you to plant what you desire in fertile soil so that you can cultivate a bountiful harvest!

All the best to your future success...

Chapter 9 Mental Tools that You Can Use to Manage Your Time Better

Learn about mental tools that you can utilize to achieve more throughout your lifetime...

If your goal is to improve your and your family's credit and finances to a "high level" it is important that you set **G**oals that are meaningful, you properly assess your **R**isks, you have adequate cash flow or **I**ncome—and you are keenly aware of your **P**ersonal Situation.

You must analyze and improve upon your:

G—oals

R—isks

I—ncome

P—ersonal Situation

If you want to improve your credit and finances **the orientation of your mind must be toward success** at all costs!

You must set "**G**oals" and never give up until you reach your goals—and then you must come up with new goals that are more challenging—and more inspiring. Whenever you set a goal, be sure to make it a point to not give up until you have accomplished that goal.

You must understand that **if you don't set goals** and strive to reach them—you are operating in fear.

If you set goals and have every intention on reaching them you are operating in courage. You must always operate in courage if your goal is to achieve at a high level. You must set goals and act upon achieving those goals in a prompt manner.

There will be many "**R**isks" that you face as you try to improve your credit and finances! However, you must take action if you want to change your life for the better! You must understand that you must act on the good ideas and visions that come into your mind. If you fail to act on the good ideas or visions that you see, you risk losing the idea or vision if you do not put the idea or vision into action.

Why Creating a Vision is so Important

Even in my own life I had visions of creating the best websites for consumers who wanted to improve their understanding of real estate, credit and finances running around in my mind for a number of years—however, those visions were nothing until I put the vision into action (put pen to pad and made it happen). The visions floated around in my mind for years and yet the vision was nothing until I took positive action.

However, once I committed my mind to create the vision—the vision had the force to change consumer behavior toward their approach to their real estate, credit and finances on a worldwide basis!

The creation "and" execution of your vision is the only thing that really counts when you really get down to it!

If you have thoughts of improving your credit and finances (or any other meaningful thoughts) and you don't act on those thoughts—those thoughts are really nothing until you take real action and make a real commitment to make those thoughts a reality.

Even if you don't know how at this present time—if you take positive action and get started you can put yourself in position to find a way to reach the goals that you desire.
You must understand that you will have to do all of the difficult things that are necessary to reach your goals.

You must visualize your successful future!

It is also important that you have adequate "Income" **or cash flow if you want to improve your credit and finances to a high level.**
You must be in financial position (or make a serious effort to get in position) to analyze and apply the powerful information in this book.
If you believe at a high level and take action at a high level, success will be in your future regardless of your past! If you utilize the knowledge that you are learning in this book you will be empowered at such a high level that success will be in your future!
You must use your inspiration to keep your flow of ideas going as it relates to your credit and finances. Your "Personal Situation" and mindset is also key to your future.

You must understand that positive change can be generated from consciousness—however, you must consciously make the choice to change your future and manifest your destiny at this moment in time and space whether your personal situation is ideal—or not so ideal!

Your unconscious mind will then have the potential to be activated at such a high level that you will be astonished at the level that thoughts and ideas begin to reach your conscious mind!
You must give serious thought to your credit and financial future consistently, study daily and plan your future on a daily or more consistent basis if you want to make the most of your abilities and achieve at a very high level!

Always have your "antennae up" for Inspiration that comes your way!

At times, you must be able to suspend your intellect or put your intellect at the back of your mind and let inspiration flow in at the front if you really want to achieve at a high level.

You must have your "receptacles" up to receive the inspiration that will come to you. You may receive inspiration unconsciously, consciously, in your dreams, and in other ways that are unknown.

The key is that you must be open to receiving the inspiration and acting on the inspiration if it is in your best interest to do so. You must not let your intelligence outwit the inspiration that you may receive as the inspiration in many cases has the power to transform your life in a major way!

Don't do like many who have access to powerful inspiration but fail to receive the inspiration and act on the inspiration. They often live their life wondering why nothing "big" is happening in their life!

It is often due to their inability to dream big and put their intelligence on the backburner or slow their mind down and receive and act on the inspiration that they receive—that truly has the potential to change their life in a major way! The creation of this chapter is the result of inspiration occurring and inspiration being acted upon.

The creation of this book is the result of dreaming big and knowing with 100% certainty that a successful completion would be the outcome!
Prior to creating this book I could have done like many and let the inspiration that entered into my mind float away possibly never to return or I could act on the inspiration just as I did—to bring you (hopefully) a better comprehension of how you can understand and apply inspiration and other mental processes in your life—to help you improve your living conditions and that of your family's!

Another mental tool that you can use that is of great value is to see your financial future with more clarity.

In the times that are now upon us all, it is imperative that you have a system of credit and finance management that provides you "clarity" and gives you the "best chance" or opportunity for success!

Isn't the time right for you to see your credit and financial future with more clarity?

You must have a clear vision of what you want to accomplish in your future and you must use that **clear vision** as a guide to make your future goals actually occur in good and bad times.

By **learning and applying the concepts that you have learned throughout this book** you should now have the **"clarity"** that is needed **"inside of your mind"** to attain and strive for your future goals at a much higher level than prior to your reading of this book!

By improving the **"clarity"** in your mind, you will take "your mind" to a higher level of thinking and you will begin to have thoughts and ideas at a higher level.

If you act on those positive thoughts and ideas that will come your way at a higher level of intensity, you will attain a higher level of success.

You want to position your mind to have a more vivid picture of what you need to do, can do and will do so that you can make real during your lifetime what you desire most. You can then live with more certainty as it relates to your building of wealth and the improvement of your financial health.

Over the years we have received countless communications from people who have used the information in this book to improve their credit and finances.

Many have taken the time to inform us that they have changed their attitude

towards their finances in large part by utilizing many of the concepts in this book.

Many have stated that they had tried to improve their credit and finances on a number of occasions in the past but found it too difficult and overwhelming until they came across many of the concepts that can be found in this book! Those communications have been inspiring and provide the fuel that continues to propel us whether by books, blogging or other sources to provide credit and finance advice at a high level. You must always remember that when it comes to improving your credit and finances, you are the only person that can stop you!

*Use that knowledge to set goals—**visualize your future—take action—work**—and **make the goals that you seek a reality** for you and your family!*

You must also remember that when you are in the process of reaching your goals you must have self-discipline, self-awareness, and self-confidence!

If you value your and your family's future you will develop and cultivate self-discipline and self-confidence at a high level. You must do so because if you are "sincere" about reaching your future credit and financial goals, you must approach those goals with the real expectation that they will be reached. You must realize that you can cultivate the habit of self-discipline or any other quality of success if you have a "real and sincere" desire to do so.

You must always have a high level of self-esteem and self-confidence regardless of how your peers or the larger society look at habits of success.

Once you cultivate the habits of success to the right level you will be able to achieve at a level and pace that you never imagined!

Always remember that every action that you take will move you closer toward your goal(s) or away from your goal(s)! To be truly successful you must apply your time and energy on things that really matter and on many occasions avoid the things that you may want to do!

Be sure to use all of the thoughts, theories, models, concepts, ideas, strategies and approaches that you are learning in this book to propel yourself and your family forward to meet the goals and objectives that you desire in the most efficient manner possible!

The insight and vision that led to the creation of this chapter was brought into existence when I made the initial decision to create this book. It is no accident that this book is totally original and written in a format that you can understand!

When you make the decision to take action on a consistent basis you set in motion the inner workings of your mind to operate at a higher level.

You too have what it takes on the inside to create the future that you desire for yourself and your family! The key is you must make a serious commitment to bring it all out!

Properly utilizing this book will assist you in gaining the "mental fortitude" or "mental strength" that is necessary for you to do the things in your credit and financial life that you need to do.

You can achieve untold success in your future! You now have access to the right information that will move you and your family forward—**if that is your desire!**

*Use that knowledge to set goals—**visualize your future, take action, work**—and **make the goals that you seek a reality** for yourself and your family!*

The creativity and vision that led to the creation of this chapter was brought into existence when I made the initial decision to begin writing over 15 years ago. It is no accident that this chapter and book are totally original and written in a style that is totally unique and a style that you have never experienced before!

It is also important that you use joy, appreciation and gratitude advantageously throughout your lifetime so that you can achieve more!

Do you know that you have the ability to create the future that you desire by utilizing your mind in an appropriate manner? You can use the emotions of joy, appreciation and gratitude that "you control" to help you stay focused and achieve at a higher level.

You can bring **"joy"** into your life and do the things that you desire most at the level that you desire if you put an **effective plan in place that allows you to achieve your goals** and **you cultivate your mental qualities** to a higher level!

As has been stated throughout this book, you must first determine where you are financially by completing a monthly budget (or cash flow statement).

By properly preparing and analyzing that statement, you can determine your fixed monthly expenses, your variable monthly expenses and you will know if you have discretionary income available that you can use for your benefit, or you will know if you are deficit spending; and therefore make plans to correct that situation and better plan for your future.

If you put together an effective plan and you take direct action on a consistent basis to make that plan happen you can achieve the success that you desire and bring the joy that you deserve into your and your family's life!

You can't live daily thinking or hoping that you will eventually get to it—you must put a plan in place that is measurable (a plan that has goals that are measurable and has a deadline for accomplishment).

Your plan must also be realistic (you must have the income and mental qualities that are needed to move forward effectively or you must be determined to get the income that is needed and cultivate the mental qualities that are needed to a higher level).

Are you waiting until the last minute to do what needs to be done on important matters in your life? Why wait until the last minute pressure? You must create that last minute pressure (urgency) on a daily basis in your own mind, even though there may be no pressure in actuality, if you are to achieve at a higher level!

You must realize that you can do much more on a daily basis! Do you realize that most people only use a fraction of their brainpower on a daily basis?

You can pay off your credit cards and other debt in a timely manner, you can take the vacation that you desire at the time that you desire, you can donate and volunteer your time to your favorite causes!

You must realize that if you are "truly sincere" you can fund your retirement account at the level that is needed for you to enjoy your retirement, and you can put yourself in position to purchase that vacation home that you always dreamed about!

You must also realize that you must "comprehend and apply" the powerful content in this book on a consistent basis.

In most cases your "consistency in action" will be the key to your financial breakthrough while utilizing this book!

You can do all the above and more!

However, it will take effort on your part!

No one can do it for you!

You must know that you are powerful, creative and you have the ability within you to get into a habit of doing what needs to be done—**NOW!**

You really are the determining factor for the future success that you desire!

You have what it takes! You must use your imagination, knowledge and intelligence to bring into existence what is necessary to bring you and your family the joy at the level that you desire!

You must understand that you can create your own opportunity!

Opportunity is all around you! You can create opportunities on your own or with others who are also creating opportunities.

However, you must decide to get started! You can begin by taking one step, but you must get started! You must move forward and you must get into the habit of taking decisive action—consistently!

Your future in large part depends on how you prepare now!

You must start now!

What is your vision for success?

What is your idea of success?

Nothing is as powerful as a vision that is "put into action" and one where you have "true faith" that the vision that you see will occur!

You must work to change who you are, right now, right where you are at if you really want to get to where you want or need to be!
You must prepare your mind for the success that you desire! By preparing your mind now you will know what to expect in your future.

You must prepare your mind now with the right knowledge so that you are ready to move to action appropriately when opportunity comes knocking!

Your daily activities and how you perceive your future will in large part determine if you are really committed!

Do you have a strategy that can take you from where you are now to where you desire or need to be so that you can enjoy life on your own terms?

A powerful vision is bigger than you and where you start. Be sure to utilize this chapter to your and your family's best advantage today!

By doing so your future will be bright, and you will **enjoy life** on your terms.

You can attain the **joy that you desire** or rejoice in knowing that you can do the things that you did in your past that brought you joy, if you put yourself in position to effectively attain your goals, you appreciate your achievements and you show gratitude for your past accomplishments and future accomplishments that lie in the horizon.

You can now use a number of strategies to address some or all areas of your credit and finances right now, with no strings attached!

Even if you are now facing a difficult stretch in your life, you must take action! Don't let life pass you by at this time because you feel the timing is not right!

You can achieve untold success in your and your family's future—starting today!

You can change your future to that of success if you look at your current position in a different way!

You can make favorable outcomes happen in your and your family's life and avoid financial strife, if you gain the preparation that you need to succeed.

You must look forward and know that the success **and joy that you desire** will come into existence for you and your family and take your living conditions higher!

The **joy that you want to bring into existence** can occur if you are truly persistent!
Don't let your mind "cave in" or be resistant!

Your success is not in the distant!

Your path to success is now...

Applying what you are reading in this book will show you how...

By living daily with **joy at your center**, having a real **appreciation for being here now** by taking the best actions possible on a consistent basis, **giving thanks or**

showing gratitude for having the ability and determination to put a serious plan for success into action and having the perseverance to follow through until the end, you are using the mental tools that you have available to your best advantage as you are on an unstoppable journey toward the success that you desire.

Your **G**oals, **R**isks, **I**ncome, and **P**ersonal situation that were discussed in this chapter were highlighted for a reason, and you want to give serious thought and analysis on how you can utilize those concepts to move forward throughout your lifetime, regardless of the season, **as you want to firmly GRIP your future** and never feel unsure.

You now have an unrelenting approach toward success—and you now have the essential knowledge that you need to achieve at a level that is your absolute best.

All the best to a lifetime of success...

Chapter 10 Tying it All Together and Using Your Action Mindset that you **NOW** have and **must use** to Build Wealth More Efficiently Throughout Your Lifetime

Learn how you can achieve meaningful and significant goals if you are sincerely willing to expend more effort and take real action to achieve success at a level that is your absolute best...

You can aim high or you can aim low, you are the one who can control your aim, as you are the one in control of how you feel about yourself and the direction that your life can, and will take!

Did you know that you are worth what you think you are worth and you can set goals that are meaningful and significant or you can set mediocre goals that will not take you where you need to be?

Currently, consumers are being pulled in many different directions when it comes to their credit and finances.

Mixed messages are often sent by many. So how do you decipher through all the noise to find information and advice that can truly move you and your family forward during turbulent or not so turbulent times?

In the area of taxes, you consistently hear rhetoric about eliminating the IRS, creating a flat tax system and other emotionally charged language about changing the financial structure in the United States and other countries that are designed to spur the emotions that lie within you.

Whether Democrat, Independent, Non-voter, Republican or any other party affiliation—you must understand that much of what you hear is basically rhetoric and political grandstanding as neither party is serious about eliminating the IRS.

Although both parties talk about the unfairness of the IRS, it is congress who has implemented many of the rules and guidelines as it relates to adjustments, benefits, credits, deductions, exceptions, exclusions, exemptions and other tax shelters that benefit select groups of taxpayers—including themselves!

Whether you perceive your current situation to be caused by others, a lack of income, where you were born/raised or any other factor, it is important that you have a vision of your future that includes taking personal responsibility (doing what you need to do and not waiting on others to do it for you) as that has been the theme of this book!

For the most part the "actions of others" are out of your control as you either can't do anything about it, or you won't do anything about it, and those in power have no real desire to abolish the IRS or do other functions that you may feel are in the best interest of the public!

However, you can do a lot about what you have under your control and if you get your **A I M** right you can move forward in a more efficient and effective manner.

A—ttitude

I—ntellect

M—otivation

If you can get your **A I M** right (which you have absolute control over), you can pay off your outstanding consumer debt, retire in abundance, take that vacation that you always dreamed of or attain any other goal(s) or objective(s) that you and your family need or desire to achieve.

It is important that you cultivate an **A**ttitude that will lead to success on a consistent basis, and you use your brainpower (**I**ntelligence) appropriately and you stay **M**otivated at a high level!

Did you know that your **A**ttitude—or the way that you think and feel about someone or something, including how you look at and think about yourself and your finances—or a feeling or way of thinking that affects your behavior or an expression of favor or disfavor toward a person, place, thing, or event is a key factor in determining your future success in many facets of your life?

It is important that you realize that what holds most people back is that they blame others or make excuses when they themselves actually have the power to transform their situation to that of real and lasting success!

You must realize that the right *Attitude* allows you to control your outcomes and not blame others! A "mindset of personal responsibility" provides you the opportunity to manage distractions and attain the future success that you desire in all areas of your life!

If you do what you are required to do you can advance forward—whether you did or did not cause your current situation! You must have the mindset that asks—what can I do to make my dreams come true? The right *Attitude* allows you to ask that question and answer it correctly and also puts your mind and thought process on a path to take the right action on a more consistent basis!

Did you know that how you use your **I**ntelligence in terms of the many different ways that you use your logic, abstract thought, understanding, awareness, communication, learning, emotions, knowledge, memory, planning and problem solving etcetera—is a key factor in determining your future success in many facets of your life?

You possess inside the knowledge (or you will soon possess) of what you can do to make your dreams come true. By approaching your credit and finances in a more intelligent manner, you will greatly increase the odds of success in your future!

By attacking your credit and finances *intelligently* you understand fully that it is your responsibility to do what you need to do to see your way through and you realize fully that it is never to your benefit to blame others or anything outside of yourself!

What are the future goals that I desire for myself and my family?

What can I do to improve my A I M?

Did you know that the **M**otivation that lies within you is the driving force that causes you to "move to action" in a sincere manner and is a major determinant of your future success in all areas of your life?

Your Motivation for doing things causes you to optimize your well-being, minimize your physical pain and maximize your pleasure.

Your *Motivation* can also originate from your specific physical needs such as eating, sleeping or resting, and other factors!

Motivation is an inner drive to behave or act in a certain manner. Your inner conditions such as your wishes, your desires and your goals, activate you to move to action in a particular manner!

Your motivation initiates, guides and maintains goal-oriented behaviors that you now have or that you may have in your future.

Motivation is what causes you to act, whether it is getting a glass of water to reduce your thirst or reading and comprehending this book to gain the empowering knowledge that you need to succeed!

Motivation requires that you use the biological, emotional, social and cognitive forces within you that activate behavior that moves you toward what you desire.

In everyday usage, the term *motivation* is frequently used to describe *why* you would do something.

For example, you might say that you are *motivated* to master the material in this book so that you can live your life on your terms—not on the terms of creditors and others who have no real concern for your future. By doing so you can put yourself and your family in position to do what you really desire in your future!

As you pursue your goals you must never be disappointed by what you expect and you must never stop too soon as you can go further, you can push harder—your motivation must endure and you must ultimately expect success and achieve success in your future!

Who says that you've done enough or accomplished enough? Why stop now? You can go higher and higher!

The "right movement" creates positive momentum and consistent motivation and goal setting helps propel that momentum!

What goals are you motivated towards accomplishing at this time?

You must never settle too quickly for too little! You must recognize success by the works that you provide and the achievements that you attain!

Did you know that people can see your worth by the work that you do and not by what you proclaim (their eyes will be opened)?

A high level of motivation causes you to taste it and see it! Your actions and your movement toward your future goals must be so sincere that it provides all that and more!

Gifts, talents, abilities, peace, and joy--you have all of that and more within you and now is the time that you apply the knowledge of what you need to do!

You must realize that no one can make you read financial advice that is good for you, however financial advice can be made available that can provide you with what you need to succeed if you are motivated toward achievement at a high level and you sincerely want to obtain and apply empowering advice that can lead to lasting success!

What is inside of you that you can use to make your dreams come true? By having the mindset that you will take personal responsibility in all that you do, the power that is needed to transform your situation will be presented to you—if you do what you need to do!

It is important that you use adversity that you may feel is happening to you for your and your family's future benefit and you use *Motivation* to respond positively to that adversity!

It is also important to look at adversity from the vantage point that adversity is happening for you (your future benefit) as opposed to happening to you (why me)!

In this final chapter, I have tried to put together powerful information that you can learn in basic understandable English and apply in your everyday life to help you attain a very high level of lasting success and improve your A I M!

Are your goal(s) to just merely survive (living for the now) or do you desire to prosper (attaining success at a level that you can leave behind something for your heirs)?

Are you looking at new and more empowering ways of thinking and doing things or are you caught up in learning and doing things in the same manner as you did in your past because it is more comfortable to you, but not more comfortable for you?

It is important that you realize that change within your mind must occur if you are to prosper (attain a higher level of success that provides you more than merely survival) and achieve the type of success that you need to attain or the type of success that you desire to attain!

Did you know that at times what you need to do to improve your credit and finances may be difficult for your ears to hear, your eyes to see and your heart and mind to accept?

Even if you don't like hearing or seeing it, you must still timely address what needs to be addressed!

Developing your heart and mind to where it needs to be to act consistently with your finances is no walk at the beach, however it is something that you must do if you desire to make your financial dreams come true!

Setting meaningful goals and taking the right actions consistently will get you to where you need to be in a much more efficient manner than if you fail to do so!

You must get to a point where you will not make excuses! You cannot do like 90% of the population and make excuses or give reasons for their inaction—and never utilize their gift appropriately or attain their life purpose!

Isn't it time that you obtain a breakthrough in your thinking, and use that breakthrough to make great things happen in your life?

Do it not only for your benefit, but your family's and future generations yet unborn!

Isn't the time right in your life for a mental re-awakening where you operate from the vantage point of success in all that you do? Now is the time that you take action and do what will lead to success and not do what the other 90% do which in many cases only leads to survival!

By reading this book, you have much of what you need to succeed and now is the time to get it done without procrastination so that you can truly reach your destination. And it will be due in large part because you **AIMed high**, so that you could exceed the sky!

By taking the right AIM at this time, you can reach your credit and financial destination and leave a legacy for the next generation!

Be sure to put your goals in writing and be sure to **A I M** high so that you can exceed the sky!

You must always realize that you can achieve any goal as long as you believe, and as long as you approach your future with the right—**A** ttitude—**I** ntellect—and **M** otivation—or by having the right—**A I M** on a consistent basis!

By taking responsibility for your future you will improve your A I M and you won't blame others or forces that you feel are beyond your control. Quite the contrary, you know that the power to do what needs to be done rests where it should be, inside of your heart and mind!

You must always realize that you are bigger than any adversity that you have faced, are now facing or that you may face in your future!

You cannot let the adversity that you may face define you or destroy your determination and commitment level—quite the contrary, you must gain strength from the adversity that you will face and move forward in a positive and inspiring manner, and with a very high level of motivation.

By setting meaningful goals and having every intention on reaching those goals you will gain the strength that you need to really succeed!

You will position your mind to gain the knowledge needed to move in the DIRECTION where SUCCESS lives and it will be due in large part because you made the choice to **A I M** high at the right TIME!

Your goal is to give it your best as you **AIM** for a higher level of success and permanently put procrastination to rest!

Why now is the time to put forth Maximum Effort on your part

It is important that you realize that effort will be required from you if you are now serious and sincere about making your wealth building dreams come true.

And just as the author of this book has used his time for your benefit over a number of months during the chaotic and unsettling times in 2025, the information in **The Art of Essential Action** was contemplated in an effort to ensure that you and others who desire real success from this day forward have access to empowering credit and finance systems and approaches that are at your fingertips—and where implementation would not be an impediment.

However, you must do your part and go after what you sincerely desire most with a high level of effort.

While many other authors are writing political books to cash in on the political season, the author of **The Art of Essential Action** decided that now was the time to provide you and others a way to achieve wealth building success more efficiently throughout your lifetime. Not only was that objective reached but priced at under $20.00 in all versions—**The Art of Essential Action** is undoubtedly one of the best values that can be found in personal finance!

You must realize that it is your responsibility to begin and end your search for answers to your most pressing questions inside of your mind and heart, and then make the best effort possible to make what you desire most happen in real time!

Your "consistency in action" can be a major boost to helping you achieve what you desire most, once you determine that you will make the commitment that is necessary throughout your lifetime!

You must develop the habits that are necessary that provides you the ability to put forth more effort on a daily basis so that you can put into action the steps that are necessary to build wealth in a more enduring way.

In closing, the vision that you formulate, along with the three steps that have been reiterated throughout this book, can be a real boost for you if you desire to build wealth efficiently and you are willing to put forth the required effort!

By having a clear vision as it relates to your wealth-building future, you will have a more realistic outlook for success!

As the years come and go, it is important that you look within and determine in a real way what you desire to occur in your wealth building future.

Are you looking forward to a successful future and are you optimistic or pessimistic about your future?

If you at this time lack the income to reach your goals, you must put together a plan to improve upon your current position—however you won't know where you now stand if you don't take action to find out exactly where you stand.

Even though others may have a pessimistic view of their future with all of the turbulence and uncertainty that in many cases are unnecessarily created, you want to rise above the fray and plan for a better day.

You must know in certain terms that a better day is coming your way, and that is what you must say from day to day, so that you can get momentum to go your way!

You want to live daily with a clear vision and know the importance of looking ahead so that you can plan for and achieve goals that will serve your and your family's best interest so you can achieve more during turbulent times and even when calmness is in the atmosphere.

1) In order to look forward you must first know where you now stand

Do you know your financial position or is it a mystery to you? It is important that you know where you stand, and you must know what you need to do now to see where you stand. If you create a budget or cash flow statement you can determine how well or poorly you are managing your income from month to month.

By taking this step at a minimum, you are leaning forward and peeking into your future, and you can "put yourself" in position to like what you see or make the necessary adjustments if you don't like what you see!

2) In order to make progress you must plan for success

Once you know what you take in monthly and pay out monthly, you can put yourself in position for greater success by putting a written plan in place that takes you where you need or want to go.

You want to plan your credit management and other areas of your finances, so you don't leave anything to chance—now that is looking forward!

3) In order to maintain your gains, you must review to help further ensure that your dreams will come true

Once you pay off or pay down your debt (if that was part of your plan), maintain mastery over your credit and manage your finances comprehensively, you want to review on occasion to see how well or poorly you are doing. Your goal on an annual basis is to increase your net worth so that you can reach the goals that you need or desire to reach.

Whether you decide to plan for that dental work that you have been delaying, set educational goals, protect your assets by purchasing an umbrella policy, invest consistently so that you reach your retirement goals, plan for your heirs after you are no longer here, or pursue any other goal(s) that are unique to you—it is imperative that you make plans to occasionally review!

Conclusion or Key Points

Regardless of where you reside, there may be uncertainty in your personal economy and/or the larger economy at some point, and you want to find a better or more certain approach to building wealth that you can understand and carry within your heart and mind so that you don't leave anything to chance! More importantly you want to have the ability to implement your plan so that you and your family can truly benefit—not creditors and others who may not have your best interests in mind.

You want to know in definite terms that if you do **1-2-3,** you can put yourself on a path to achieving results that you can see. By taking time out of your busy schedule at this time (pun intended) you can start or continue on a journey of putting your own mind and heart in control of your wealth building and financial destiny, so that you can achieve at a level that you were meant to achieve at!

You want to know early on that wealth is a mindset, therefore you want to have a mindset that is real and one that you can sincerely utilize for your benefit throughout your life!

To attain true wealth, you want to **"look forward"** and see in yourself someone who is in serious pursuit of sound physical health, a positive mental attitude, an enthusiastic spirit, a cooperative spirit, one who is intelligent in thought, have an appreciation for life, shows loyalty to others when it is appropriate, have a mental and written plan with accountability to someone else, a pleasing personality, the ability to manage time effectively, have a big imagination, someone who gives or does more than is expected, and someone who has self-confidence and energy management that flows within appropriately as guiding principles that direct your actions throughout your life!

Even when it seems like a constant stream of negativity is in the atmosphere that will never end, by **looking forward** and **making a commitment to do more-**-you can glide forward, rise higher and truly soar!

You want to know at all times that you have “effective control over your mind” and in a real sense that is true wealth, however it is not monetary in nature in and of itself. You have the power within and without, to do more and achieve more by having a vision of your future that allows you to soar.

Always realize that "taking the right action" is a big part of the equation and you can use the power of persuasion to improve your situation and continue on a path toward success throughout your lifetime.

And even as you view your future with more certainty and achieve at a high level, you want to at the same time ensure that you have balance in your life, as by having the right balance that will propel you forward even more!

Your "success" or "failure" in achieving your goals are in large part determined by **your mental approach that you utilize consistently throughout your lifetime**, your goals, risk level, income and personal situation—and it is you who in many cases control those variables and how tight you want to **GRIP** (grasp) those variables.

In a final attempt to get you to achieve more, **The Art of Essential Action** will metaphorically leave you with a poem:

Pain All Over

I'm in pain from head to toe

However, despite my pain, I know where I need to go

I know that I can't live in financial strife

I know that I must move forward at all stages of my life

I know that I am in pain from head to toe

However, I will still achieve results that will show

I'm in pain all over, yet I move like a rover

For I know wholeheartedly that what I am pursuing will come true

I now know in definite terms that "I" must do what I need to do

In the process of pursuing it all at a level that is the best that is within me

I then realized—that the pain is over, and now I can clearly see

When it comes to improving your finances always remember you can use a cash flow statement, mastery of your credit and a "real understanding of what you can do to manage your finances comprehensively" to move along in life in a more joyous and rewarding way and at the same time achieve the results that you desire.

You must make it a priority to properly establish an emergency fund at the earliest time possible and reduce your and your family's financial risks.

You can do all that and more and achieve more–starting today!

It is very important that you make good use of your time, and you put in the required effort (action) to make what you desire to occur in your future happen more efficiently for your and your family's greater benefit!

Over the years many consumers have asked, what will it take for me to achieve the results that I desire in my future?

The answer always depends on your current knowledge base—your money management personality and where you are now at in your credit and financial life, along with the goals that you are in pursuit of!

If you have low or negative discretionary income, outstanding credit card debt, and many areas of your finances that need to be addressed, it will take more effort on your part than those who are not in that position.

Regardless of where you are now at you must come to the realization that it will take effort on your part if you desire to achieve meaningful and significant goals!

This book is the result of imagining and creating a wealth building book that adds value to your life, and a book that was designed to help you unlock and achieve your potential in your life so that success can overflow in your life.

Furthermore, this book is about helping you obtain the mental working knowledge that allows you to share that knowledge with your loved ones and others.

Your goal is to take in information and advice that will lead to positive results that you can benefit from and share with others, and your goal should be to also prepare your mind with what you need to know, so that you can succeed on a consistent basis and truly grow.

It is very important at this time to realize in clear terms that you must make good use of your time and you must put in the required effort if you desire efficiency in attaining meaningful goals in your and your family's future!

You must think, plan and come up with strategies for your future success that will truly lead to the success that you desire.

What You Must Do Now to Make Your Dreams Come True

You must plan—do—and review—if you desire to make your dreams come true!

You must come up with the right strategy that will do what it needs to do in order to help prevent bad things from happening to you.

You must make a difference while you are here on earth and make your life count—and truly show your worth!

You must have the mindset that you will put in the required effort that is needed so that you can live your future with a high level of persistence and not live your future on the terms of creditors and others who could care less about your existence.

You must grow daily in all areas of your life and improve in your knowledge of your finances and you must know what you can and need to do as you improve your current circumstances.

You must be open to new ideas in the area of personal finance and you must expand your thought horizon exponentially!

It is also important that you expose your mind to a more excellent way of managing your personal finances on a daily basis, much of which you have already learned in this book.

You must listen to, read about and view the best material available in personal finance and choose among the best strategies that you feel will work for you and your family.

Doing all of the above requires effort on your part, but it is required if you desire to achieve at a very high level in your and your family's financial future in the times that we now live in!

Putting in the required effort means that you will make the best use of your time, commitment, determination, focus and other positive qualities of success on a consistent basis.

Now is the time that you supercharge your mind and use this book to give your finances a new look!

Your reading of this book may have occurred in order to give you the direction that you may need so that you can truly succeed at this point in your life.

If you have the potential to succeed you must do so as you can't depend on others to do it for you!

By getting to this final chapter, you are now in position to succeed in all areas of your credit and finances, however actually doing so is up to you, your choice—your decision!

If you are serious about your and your family's future, you will not retreat and you will not move in the opposite direction of where you need to go!

You must dig deeper, push harder and reach higher toward the success that you desire at this time in your life!

You must be forthright in your approach, and you must operate with a system that is designed to do what it was intended to do.

You must also utilize a system that will help you attain the success that you desire in the most efficient and effective manner possible!

You must always realize that when you are empowered to do good and do what is righteous, you should do good and what is righteous!

This book is designed to lift you up, not tear you down.

And provide you the ability to reach back and bring up those who may be on the wrong path—financially speaking, and put them on the same upward path to success that you now have the opportunity to take!

You can achieve success and be a blessing for others in spite of whether you are now attaining major success or financial difficulty is now occurring in your life.

Regardless of what you are going through or what you have been through, success can now happen for you!

You can be more than an enabler! You can now reach back and help others in an empowering manner if you first get your house in order at this time!

This book was created for those who want to build a strong credit and finance foundation and achieve at a very high level in the current economy or any economy.

How will you handle adversity that will undoubtedly come your way?

Are you a change agent or are you one who operates in theory only?

When difficult times occur in your life you must get into the habit of taking the right action in real time to make what you really desire occur. And you must realize upfront that it will take major effort on your part to do so!
Passion, commitment, creativity, action, work that empowers, that is what it takes!

Your ultimate goal should be to have an impact in the lives of others!

No one will remember you by what your material possessions are, but they will remember you by the imprint that you made in their life!

Your "decisive action" at this time can lead you toward effective wealth building throughout your lifetime.

When it comes to reaching meaningful and significant goals that you "really" want to achieve, it is important that you have a decisive mindset if you sincerely desire to achieve those goals.

And when it comes to building wealth efficiently it is more important than ever that you are "decisive" in your decision to pursue what you desire most at your highest level of effort and energy.

It is also critical that you know the importance of "being decisive" when it comes to building wealth and pursuing your goals in a manner that is more beneficial for you and your family. You want to ensure at the earliest time possible that you cultivate a decisive mindset, take decisive action when appropriate and have the determination to make what you desire occur, all of which will be discussed in more detail below.

Decisive Mindset

It is important that you have a "made up mind" when it comes to building wealth more efficiently.

It is important that you run through your mind in a serious manner what it is that you really believe, and you really want to achieve.

You must know that success lives in you—because if you sincerely know this—you put one of the most important ingredients necessary (that can lead you toward making your dreams come true) in the mix and that can be the needed ingredient that can give your finances a needed fix or boost!

You must know in certain terms that you are responsible for achieving the results that you want to see and you must have the mental fortitude that is stronger than a palm tree.

Decisive Action

It takes more than just a mindset of decisiveness to get things done—you must also move to action toward what you desire to occur in a consistent manner.

You must act on what you know can move you forward and not just let what can move you forward exist in your mind. Your daily habits and "consistency in action" is what will give you real traction.

When you really think about it, your thoughts or plans that you have are really nothing!

It is only when you take action and put into motion what you know you need to do to turn those thoughts into something (the goals that you desire or need to achieve) that you want to see come true, that you will reach significant goals.

Decisive Determination

You must have an unrelenting spirit to pursue what you desire at a level that is the best that is within you and at a level that allows you to do what you need to do to make your dreams come true.

Even if you have the mental toughness and you plan on taking action on a consistent basis, that alone will not be enough if you are not determined or determined at a really high level.

You must put into motion what you need to do, "and" you must also be determined at a high level to always take what you are pursuing in as serious a manner as possible, if you have every intention of achieving what you desire.

There is no reason for you to be upset (**MAD**) about your current state of your finances regardless of your current financial condition, and there is no reason for you to "fear your wealth building future" if you possess in your **m**ind the right tools and you use those tools to your best **a**dvantage at the various stages **d**uring your life.

You must have the right **m**indset, take the right **a**ction and **d**etermine at this time that you truly want success in your future!

It is also important that you know your money management personality at this time and then take action and choose to improve upon your personality by taking the necessary steps in a determined manner (starting right now) as by doing so that will allow you to achieve in a more definite and more efficient manner.

Why leave your future to chance when you can put in place steps that can take you toward your destiny and who you were truly meant to be while you are here on planet earth?

You must give it your best and take decisive action to work toward achieving a higher level of success.

You want to look within, give deep thought, ponder, examine, observe, analyze and take into account and consider whether you really are willing to put forth the effort that is needed or you are determined to get to a point where you will—so that you will do what you need to do!

As you pursue your goals you also want to understand that compassion, direction and correction work on everyone's behalf!

You must pursue your credit and financial goals with the real expectation that the goals that you seek in your credit and financial life will "really occur" in your life!

You must pursue your credit and financial goals with real passion and you must really want to achieve the goals that you set deep down in your heart (your intellect, will and emotions must really be involved at a high level) after you have given serious thought to the goals that you want to achieve!

When you are operating in a sincere manner you can more effectively direct your future!

When you are operating with "true sincerity" towards your credit and financial goals you can see the vision (your goals) occurring and you can feel it happening.

You have no doubt that what you are seeking will really occur because you are pursuing your goals at such a high level and you have the preparation and knowledge that is necessary (much of which you have learned in this book) that success is the only outcome that is possible!

You cannot deceive yourself! You must pursue your goals with a very high belief that the goals that you seek will occur!

Pursuing success at your highest level is a quality that you must cultivate if your goal is to truly transform your credit and financial life!

You must believe in your "mind and heart" that your journey of credit and finance improvement will really occur and will get you the wealth building results that you and your family desire.

You can pay off or pay down your current outstanding debt in a timely manner! You can purchase organic food from the top grocery retailers!

You can take that vacation that you know you deserve! You can fund your retirement accounts at the right level!

You can have discretionary income on a monthly basis at the level that you desire so that you can pursue other goals and dreams that you and your family may have!

However you must put a workable written plan together and gain an understanding of how credit and finances work in a better way—if your goal is to achieve at a very high level from day to day!

Your effort level will show in your daily activities and how you apply what you are learning in this book.

If you apply the information in this book at a high level and in a **sincere manner**, success will be the only outcome that is possible!

You can now take your credit and finances in the direction that you desire—not the direction that your creditors desire.

Be sure to use all of the empowering information in this book that you feel can move you forward to truly transform your credit and financial future from this day forward!

Always remember that if your goal is to succeed at a high level you must make a serious commitment and you must be **"truly sincere"** in your efforts to improve your credit and finances while you pursue your goals!

By doing so you can start on a path that will lead to a more rewarding and uplifting lifestyle for yourself and your family, from this day forward!

You can no longer blame your lack of resources (whether financial or educational), justify your inaction by making excuses or stating in your mind that you don't know what to do.

On a daily basis you can know what you need to do and continue your journey toward making all your dreams come true!

Are you currently "sincere" about your future success?

Why would you at this time decide to do less, when you can make the choice to give it your best?

Now is the time that you ignite your own fire—inside your mind and heart—and achieve the type of success that will truly set you apart!

You are the **spark** that that you have been looking to see and **you are the one** who must achieve and be all that you were sincerely meant to be!

Untold success lies ahead in your credit, finances, and life for you, your family and your loved ones, if you put in the required effort on a consistent basis!

Reading **The Art of Essential Action** today has hopefully shown you a highly effective way!

Major success for you and your family can now happen and in the end it will be you and your family who will truly win, **as you have the essence of what is needed to take the necessary action**, so that you can achieve the wealth building and other goals that you desire most, and live out your life on your terms from coast to coast.

Always remember that pray and wait—your results may not be great, however pray and action will lead to a higher level of satisfaction and put you in position to move forward with the right traction. You want to utilize an authentic, bold, confident, and daring approach if you desire to achieve more as you navigate life, even when the intricacies of life appear very complicated or detailed.

You can achieve a lifetime of success by taking “essential action” and building wealth in a style and format that works with your mind and not against it. You now have a new thought pattern that you can use to build wealth throughout your lifetime.

You are now in position to lead your life (plan proactively with confidence) and not let your life lead you (be pulled in directions that do not serve your best interest). You are now in position to see your future with more clarity and lift others as you climb higher.

When you plan your financial future, you want to think ahead in concrete terms as well as abstract terms as what will and can happen (adversity) often won't be laid out for you in black and white and give you advanced notice.

The pressures that you face daily from this day forward will hopefully force you to operate in your **purpose** and lead to you achieving meaningful goals throughout your lifetime.

You no longer must imagine knowing the steps that you can take, and particularly the 3-step structured approach that you have learned in this book that allows you the opportunity to build wealth throughout your life in more definitive ways. Even if you feel you don't have the **3-step structured approach** fully mastered at this time, **Appendix B** will provide you with even more clarity and further position you for a lifetime of success.

As a more informed money manager, you have shifted the power in your favor and you will have a serious posture when you meet with financial and other professionals throughout your lifetime.

It is important to realize that "what you allow" whether positive or negative will continue, therefore you want to impose the power source that you have within, so that you can win!

You must put a demand on the positive qualities that may be lying dormant in you at this time so those thoughts (qualities) are dominant, and you must have the mindset that you will use your energy for "moving forward with action" as opposed to wasting your energy on things that don't really matter.

All the best as "you" visualize your future, plan for and achieve unlimited success, *look forward* and "take essential action" at a level that is your absolute best...

Appendix A

Other books by Thomas (TJ) Underwood

Book 1) Managing & Improving Your Credit & Finances for this MILLENNIUM©2012

Book 2) HOME BUYER 411 *The Smart Guide to Buying Your Home*©2014, updated 2023

Book 3) HOME SELLER 411 *The Smart Guide to Selling Your Home*©2014, updated 2023

Book 4) The Wealth Increaser©2014, updated 2023

Book 5) The FIZBO Manual©2014, updated 2023

Book 6) 1-2-3 Credit & Me©2021, updated 2023

Book 7) The 3 Step Structured Approach to Managing Your Credit & Finances ©2014, updated ©2023—amazon release in June

Book 8) Credit & Finance Improvement Made Easy ©2014, 2023—amazon release in August

Book 9) Wealth Building AXIOMS Volume 1©2024

Book 10) Wealth Building Now ©2024—amazon release in April

Book 11) Taxing Subject Matters Made Easy ©2025—amazon release in May

Book 12) The Art of Essential Action ©2026—amazon release in November

Thomas (TJ) Underwood has created over 700 pages of credit, finance, and wealth building articles covering the entire spectrum of personal finance on three websites. He is also the Author of over 10 books that are part of **The Real Estate & Finance 360 Degrees Series of Books©** that are designed **to help consumers achieve success in an intelligent, consistent and proactive** manner.

He considers it an honor to use his rare combination of experience as a former fee-only financial planner, former top-producing loan processor and current position as an active real estate broker serving the Atlanta Metropolitan area to provide readers enlightening personal finance systems and approaches that they can implement in their life that will provide them the opportunity to achieve what they truly desire in the most efficient and effective manner possible.

The creation of numerous books over the past 15 years has brought forth a new version of financial planning that turns the odds in your favor (not creditors) and more importantly puts you in control of your finances and wealth building activity in a way that could lead to greater success for you and your family throughout your lifetime.

In the **preceding chapters,** you have learned about "action behavior" that can transform your life if applied appropriately, and the material can help you achieve your credit/financial (and life) goals at a higher level "in this and the coming decades" while you are here on planet earth.

Be sure to visit the following sites to enhance your tax and wealth building knowledge and achieve even more throughout your lifetime:

***TheWealthIncreaser.com *Realty-1-Strategic-Advisors.com and**

***The-best-atlanta-real-estate-advice.com**

Appendix B

The 3 Step Structured Approach (A Comprehensive Financial Management System)

In easy-to-understand format, you must know how to:

1) Utilize personal finance statements appropriately

1. Establish a personal **b**udget or cash flow statement at a minimum
2. Create a personal **i**ncome statement
3. Create a personal **b**alance sheet
4. Create a personal **n**et worth statement

2) Gain mastery of how you manage your credit

Negative information must be kept off of your credit report

Utilization of your available credit must be at a reasonable level

Time of open accounts is important

Types of accounts are important

Inquiries must be kept at a reasonable level

3) Comprehensively understand your finances in the following areas

Insurance

Investments

Taxes

Emergency fund

Education planning

Estate Planning/Wills

Retirement planning

By just being **exposed to** the **3 steps** above--you are far ahead of the average consumer who for the most part has no real understanding of what personal finance encompasses—let alone the ability to use the knowledge of what personal finance encompasses to their and their family's greater benefit.

What you need to do financially

Now that you have knowledge of what you need to know (pun intended) **you must take the right steps** and put into action the results of your cash flow statement or budget at a minimum. Whether you have a monthly surplus or a monthly deficit you are now in position for more effective planning from this point forward.

If you are comfortable with numbers, you may also want to create an income statement and balance sheet so that you can determine your net worth at this time—and improve upon your net worth in the coming years.

The creation of a "properly funded emergency fund" will go a long way in helping you increase your net worth in future years!

You must also gain mastery over how you manage your credit by knowing how to **utilize your knowledge of the 5 credit factors**—as that knowledge can prevent you from getting into a difficult financial hole where climbing out is difficult or highly unlikely (you may need to consider filing bankruptcy as a real option).

Finally, you must know how to select the appropriate insurance products and investment options along with doing, education planning, estate planning and retirement planning in a manner that is more advantageous for you and your family—not creditors or others who have no real concern for your lasting success.

The importance of reviewing what you do financially

Now that you have a comprehensive overview of your finances and you have been **exposed** to all that you need to know (and do) to work toward making your wealth building goals come true, you "must" be aware of your need to review!

You must review your personal finance statements, including your emergency fund to make sure you are adequately protected. You must review your understanding of the 5 credit factors so that you can make the right or at a minimum, good decisions as it relates to your use of credit.

You must review your insurance, investments, taxes, education planning, estate planning/wills, and retirement planning on a routine basis to see where improvements can be made.

Regardless of your past experiences, the environment in which you grew up in and the positive or negative exposures in your life, you are now in position to change all of that to your advantage—and by being **exposed to personal finance** in a way that you can readily understand and utilize, you are now ready to take your prize.

It is important that you are **exposed to all areas of financial planning** that you need to do throughout your life at the earliest possible time. By doing so you can get out in front of potential disruptions and "proactively plan your future" in a manner that is more advantageous for you and your family.

You can put yourself in position where you can live with confidence and the success that you desire will not only occur—it will be expected. You no longer need to approach your financial future with doubt, uncertainty, and a feeling of "can't do"—as by purchasing this book you have positioned yourself in a major way to make your dreams come true.

All the best because of your willingness to be "exposed to financial systems" that can lead to lasting success.

The 3 Step Structured Approach to Improving Your Credit & Finances®

Step 1

BIB N

You can easily remember BIB N

B—stands for Budgeting or Cash Flow Statement

I—stands for Income Statement

B—stands for Balance Sheet

N—stands for Net Worth Statement

The above statements are all personal finance statements, and you will need to create and analyze each one. Be sure to be as accurate as possible with the data you enter.

Once analyzed, you will have to determine ways that you can improve each statement and then come up with a written plan of action for improving each statement so that your financial ratios and net worth will move in the right direction.

Step 2

Remember **NUTTI** or **MUTTI** in your GUTTI to improve your credit score forevermore.

This too, you can also easily remember:

N stands for Negative Information—**M** is for Messed Up—if either occur, your credit will be highly affected as this generally makes up 35% of your credit score.

U stands for Utilization or how you use your credit, and it too is very important as this generally makes up to 30% of your credit score.

T stands for Time and is another important factor as you should keep older accounts open and always pay on time. Just as "i" in time comes before "y" in type, time comes before type when you are memorizing this acronym. Time generally makes up to 15% of your credit score.

T stands for Type and it comes after time. The types of credit you have are important as a good mix is better than no mix. If you have several credit cards, a home loan, and an auto loan that would be a better type of credit than just having several credit cards. The type of credit makes up to 10% of your credit score.

I stands for Inquiries and you should keep your inquiries low if you will be seeking new credit and/or are attempting to improve your credit score. Inquiries also make up to 10% of your credit score.

Note the descending order of the percentages above are:

N or **M** = 35%

U = 30%

T = 15%

T = 10%

I = 10%

Total 100%

Remembering in that order will also help structure the acronym so keep the percentages along with what each acronym represents fresh in your mind.

If your credit is unsatisfactory at this stage, you will have to clean up your credit and work on getting your credit position to an acceptable level so that you can reach your future goals and objectives.

Step 3

My Eyes Tear

My Eyes Tear when I see that my financial future is clear.

The above sentence is a play on words and the memory triggering aspect is:

Your eyes would represent the (**ii's**).

Your tear would represent the (**teeer**) in the following acronym.

The first **(I)** represents your Insurance Planning

The second (**I**) represents your Investment Planning

The (**T**) represents your Tax Planning

The first (**E**) represents your Emergency Fund

The second (**E**) represents your Education Planning

The third (**E**) represents your Estate Planning/Wills

The (**R**) represents your Retirement Planning

You will have to analyze each area of your finances and see what you need to do immediately and, in your future, to improve your position. You should also know at this point what you will need to do in the future as you may not be in financial position now to address all of your financial concerns.

However, you should be aware at this stage of what you need to do in "all areas" of your finances.

Now, do you think you can cultivate a mental framework or mindset that includes the **3 steps above**? Of course you can!

OK, Let's Review

- **BIB N** stands for...
- Remember **NUTTI or MUTTI** in your GUTTI to improve your credit score forevermore and each letter in **NUTTI and MUTTI** stand for...and the percentage in each letter stand for...
- **My EYES TEAR** when I realize my financial future is clear and **your eyes are your (ii's)** and **your tear are your (teeer)** and each letter stands for...

Recite it in your mind until all of the "3 Steps" become second nature to you. Don't get too concerned about the deeper understanding of each letter at this time as they will come to you if you navigate realty-1-strategic-advisors.com and/or you purchase **Managing & Improving Your Credit & Finances for this MILLENNIUM**—our new book.

It will all come together for you by navigating **TheWealthIncreaser.com**—our most recent blog site.

With just what you have just learned you put yourself ahead of most consumers when it comes to the effective understanding of personal finance.

This is only the beginning of your journey to financial freedom. Just mastering and understanding the 3 steps listed above are well worth the price you paid for this book as you now have the essentials of what you can do in your future to attain lasting success.

Open your mind, ears, and eyes wide as we go into deeper detail of how you utilize **The "3 Step Approach" to Managing & Improving Your Credit & Finances** in your and your family's life—today!

Get your "mindset" to the point where for the rest of your life you will always know:

BIB N—Remember **NUTTI or MUTTI** in your GUTTI to improve your credit score forever more—and my **EYES TEAR** when I realize my financial future is clear.

Once you have the above acronyms solidly memorized you will be well on your way to living your life in a manner that suits you and your family best—not your creditors.

Be sure to comprehend the above acronyms at your highest level. In other words, open your mind, ears, and eyes wide and put on your thinking cap.

In this short appendix, you have the opportunity to master your understanding of credit and finance in a style and manner rarely seen—in personal finance.

This book was intentionally written in a somewhat entertaining and engaging style with serious content that was designed to get your mind to open up.

By reading this short book you should now be in great position to apply the information and change your and your family's financial condition for generations.

Final thoughts on the 3 Step Structured Approach

It is critical that you have the proper understanding, and you know how to properly apply the helpful acronyms that you have learned.

You must at all times know:

1)

that you need to properly create and analyze your **B**udget or Cash Flow—so that you know your inflow and outflow of cash on a monthly basis.

Even if you decide to create an **I**ncome Statement, **B**alance Sheet Statement and **N**et Worth Statement later—you need to create at a minimum a Budget or Cash flow Statement—at this time!

2)

Your understanding and application of Remember **NUTTI** or **MUTTI** in your GUTTI to improve your credit score forevermore.

Improving Your Credit Score in a Nutshell

Remember **NUTTI or MUTTI** in your GUTTI to maximize your credit SCORE, FOREVERMORE!

Follow me here...It will make sense...I promise...

N---"Negativity"---try to avoid negative information in your payment history---35% of your score

U---keep "Utilization" and amount owed low---keep debt low---30% of your score

T---always pay on "Time," keep old accounts open---15% of your score

T---keep a good mix and have different “Types” of credit---10% of your score

I---keep "Inquiries” low by loan shopping within a small window---10% of your score

Or Another Way to Look At It

M---don’t “Mess up” your credit---try to avoid “negative info” on your report---35%

U---keep “Utilization” at a low percentage of your total debt---keep debt low---30% of your score

T---always pay on “Time,” keep old accounts open---15% of your score

T---keep a good mix and “Type” of credit---10% of your score

I---keep “Inquiries” for the last 12 months low if you will be seeking new credit---10% of your score

Did you know that I set you up for a short catchy Acronym (although somewhat strange) that has the potential to help you take control of your credit for the rest of your life?

If you memorize and utilize the following phrase in the right manner, you will be in position to improve your credit position. Feel free to pass it along to your family and friends to help them improve their credit score and credit situation as well.

Although the Acronym (memory trigger) is somewhat “weird” you should easily remember it for the rest of your life by reciting it in your mind on a constant basis—until you are confident that you have it memorized, and you understand the underlying concepts behind the acronym.

Remember NUTTI or MUTTI in your GUTTI to maximize your credit SCORE, FOREVERMORE!

By simply memorizing the preceding Acronym and utilizing the knowledge gained—you can take positive control of your financial situation—and that of your loved ones. OK—one last time...

N stands for ... and M stands for... 35% of your score

U stands for... and U stands for...30% of your score

T stands for... and T stands for...15% of your score

T stands for... and T stands for...10% of your score

I stands for... and I stands for...10% of your score

OK, your time is up, I'm sure you have all the factors that go into maintaining and improving your credit and credit score mastered.

It is also important that you realize that there are two major scoring models:

1) **FICO score**
2) **VantageScore**

If you utilize the five factors above appropriately, you will have a good to excellent credit score regardless of the model that is being used. Always realize that newer models, older models, industry specific models and other models are on the market at the same time and the calculation of your scores will vary depending on the model used by the creditor or the entity requesting your score!

Furthermore, you should know that there are 3 major credit bureaus:

1) **TransUnion**
2) **Equifax**
3) **Experiean**

An easy way to remember the 3 major credit bureaus is to think that you will be TEEing off—however it won't be for golf—but for improving your credit and credit score!

The above structuring technique brings clarity to help you improve and maintain you credit for the rest of your life. By simply remembering the weird poem or statement—you put yourself in a position to always know what you need to do to improve and maintain your credit.

It is also important that you realize that consumers who must be concerned about the FCRA (Fair Credit Reporting Act) and other corrective credit improvement systems—normally are those who have mismanaged their credit in the past.

It is imperative that you manage and improve your credit and finances in a **more intelligent, consistent, and proactive manner**—in order to avoid getting into a credit position that is adverse for you and your family!

You can choose to learn other creative ways or even learn the FCRA standards and guidelines and other systems of credit and finance management if you choose too—however we do not believe you will find a more effective and efficient system than "Remember **NUTTI or MUTTI** in your GUTTI to improve your credit score forevermore"—that you have learned in this precise and to the point guide.

However, do not use our beliefs **as an excuse** to not do your due diligence and determine for yourself if there is a better system or approach that is available that will work better for you and your family.

It is imperative that you use your intelligence to analyze other credit and finance systems in an **analytical, accurate, careful and critical manner** and decide for yourself what works best for you and your family!

If you comprehend and master the use of "Remember **NUTTI or MUTTI** in your GUTTI to improve your credit score forevermore"—you will primarily have what you need—to succeed when it comes to managing and improving your credit for the rest of your life.

It is important that you realize that the **"3 Step Approach"** and the Credit Improvement system mentioned above will essentially provide you with what you need once you get your credit properly established.

If you desire a comprehensive system that can move you forward on a continuous basis—you have found that with the "3 Step Approach."

Therefore, don't get too uptight or concerned about your credit as long as you have a thorough understanding, and you know how to apply in a practical manner (and you actually do so)—"Remember **NUTTI or MUTTI** in your GUTTI to improve your credit score forevermore."

Be sure you understand and remember the **ratio percentages** for each letter as by doing so you will be well ahead of 90% of the population when it comes to the understanding and application of credit. And having the ability to maintain and increase your credit score on a consistent basis is an important skill set that you can pass along to others.

Be sure that you understand that different jargon may be spoken or written regarding the credit factors mentioned above, and it is your responsibility to understand that jargon.

By mastering the **"3 Step Approach"** you will even have a more effective and efficient practical system of credit and finance management and understanding than many professionals who work in the financial industry.

You can choose to waste or perhaps not waste your time by learning about the FCRA (Fair Credit Reporting Act), CFPB (Consumer Finance Protection Bureau), USA.gov—and other credit resources that may add more confusion and frustration than lasting results, or you can choose to know and use "Remember **NUTTI or MUTTI** in your GUTTI to improve your credit score forevermore"—and use the knowledge that you have gained in a manner where you will apply what you have learned to manage and improve your credit in a more stress-free, effective, efficient and results oriented manner!

You must always remember that your worthiness, character, capacity, and general reputation plays a major factor in your credit score. It is important that you choose to **"properly focus"** and leave excuses behind—and by comprehending and applying "Remember **NUTTI or MUTTI** in your GUTTI to improve your credit score forevermore" on a consistent basis you can put yourself in position to manage your credit effectively for years to come.

You also should know that by mastering "Remember **NUTTI or MUTTI** in your GUTTI to improve your credit score forevermore"—that does not preclude you from learning additional credit systems and approaches if you have a desire to do so.

However, you must realize that it is truly not necessary for your and your family's future success if you operate in a proactive (gain the knowledge that you need NOW—by using the above acronym in a way that is most beneficial to your credit usage or anticipated credit usage) manner!

It is important that you realize that the amount of credit that is made available to you is often based on the income that you earn in your household and other factors.

It is also important that you realize that your failure to understand how to manage your credit and finances is your choice and you must further realize that you are responsible for not only your future success, but the success of your family and other loved ones as well!

If you have an established and functional **(mental working knowledge)** system of attacking your credit and finances, you can more precisely and more accurately determine what lies ahead (plan better) for you and your family in the financial realm of your and your family's life!

You must live your life purposely and with a real willingness to achieve what you desire!

A **comprehensive system of approaching your credit and finances** leaves nothing to chance—and is an approach that those who truly desire success utilize on a consistent basis!

3)

The final structuring technique in the **"3 Step Approach"** that can help you improve your finances is listed below.

My EYES TEAR

- My eyes tear when I see that my financial picture is clear.
- My eyes tear when I see that my financial independence is near.
- My eyes tear when all my credit card balances disappear.
- My eyes tear when I realize I have no financial fear.
- My eyes tear when I know that I have succeeded this year.

If you were to look at the above poem on the surface it would have some meaning to you. However, the real power of the poem lies beneath the surface—and when properly applied could easily change your mindset or the way that you look at finance in general.

Acronyms can play a key role in simplifying complex problems and can make the mind work easier and eliminate or reduce your stress levels.

In the above poem your **eyes** are your (**ii's**) and your **tears** are your (**teeer**). Let me explain further so that you have a clear understanding.

The above poem is a "play on words." In your financial life you should be concerned with your **i**nsurance and **i**nvestments or another way of looking at it, your **eyes** (**ii**).

In your financial life you should also be concerned with your **t**axes, **e**mergency fund, **e**ducation planning, **e**state planning/wills, and **r**etirement planning or another way of looking at it, your **tear** (**teeer**).

- By simply remembering the poem above or simply the title of the poem—you bring clarity to your financial understanding immediately.
- By reciting the poem or a line in the poem **daily, weekly, monthly or whatever time frame you prefer** you get to a point where you know <u>all of the areas of your finances that you need to address immediately</u>—thus reducing your stress level or unhealthy concern about your finances.

- Used in conjunction with **BIB N**, Remember **NUTTI or MUTTI** in my GUTTI to improve my credit score forevermore—**my eyes tear** when I see that my financial picture is clear has the real effect of **"you knowing all of the areas of your finances that you must address"** at the drop of a hat.
- This alone would greatly reduce the stress in your life and give you a feeling of well-being in your financial realm for the rest of your life—**particularly after you address and improve each area to the maximum effect possible based on your financial condition**—and you can address those areas more appropriately at this time by going to realty-1-strategic-advisors.com—NOW—and/or purchasing **Managing & Improving your Credit & Finances for this MILLENNIUM**!
- Although what you have just learned are simple concepts—by reciting and understanding the concepts behind what the acronyms stand for, you have immediately brought clarity to your credit and financial life and that alone would put you well ahead of the general population as far as understanding your credit and finances.
- You have just had the opportunity to master these life-changing acronyms, keep them in the forefront of your mind as you go through life—as by doing so you will improve your and your family's credit and financial future well-being—quite significantly!

Can you believe that a **"3 Step Approach"** that utilizes **7 words—**has provided the mental framework that allows you to know in a **comprehensive manner what you need to do for the rest of your life** to manage your credit and finances in a highly effective and efficient manner?

However, don't take the above statement at face value! You must seriously ask yourself—do I have a system that does the above, or do I know of a system that does?

BONUS SECTION: Investment Simplification & Wealth Building

Learn how you can at this time choose the right investment vehicle(s) to effectively reach your investment goals...

It is important that you start your long-term investing at the earliest time possible and there are investment vehicles that you can utilize to get you where you need to be more efficiently.

In this bonus section you will learn some of the most useful and time-tested investment vehicles that you can use to build wealth and reach goals that you desire at the various stages of your life.

Your path to **investment success** does not have to be a difficult one if you start early, invest consistently and you know your "target number" that you need to reach to fulfill your various goals.

Your home purchase, college funding, traveling around the world, reaching your retirement number or reaching the number that you need to reach for any other purpose is attainable if you are at this time willing to make a serious effort toward achieving what you desire.

Mutual Funds (MFs)

A **Mutual fund** is an investment program funded by shareholders that trades in diversified holdings and is professionally managed. It normally includes a "bundle of stocks" and investment products and frees you from the hassle of selecting individual stocks or other investments yourself.

A **MF** is a portfolio of stocks, bonds and other securities and creates a diversified investment portfolio that generally reduces your risk factor. It is key that you understand that mutual funds are "**bought and sold**" at the "**end of**" the trading day!

- Mutual funds are sold based on dollars, so "**you can specify any dollar amount**" that you'd like to invest.

- Mutual funds are divided into several kinds of categories, representing the kinds of securities they invest in, their investment objectives, and the type of returns they seek. Although there are others, most mutual funds fall into categories which include **stock** funds, **money market** funds, **bond** funds, and **target-date** funds.

- Mutual funds charge annual fees, expense ratios, or commissions, which may affect their overall returns and you want to ensure that the fund that you select has reasonable fees.

- Employer-sponsored retirement plans commonly invest in mutual funds and if your employer offers them—especially with an employee match, you want to put yourself in position to contribute as best you can, based on your financial ability to do so.

Index Funds (IFs)

Technically a Mutual Fund, **Index funds** invest in stocks that correspond with a major market index such as the S&P 500, Nasdaq or the Dow Jones Industrial Average (DJIA). It could be one focused on a sector, such as healthcare, durable goods or technology. This investment strategy requires less research from analysts and advisors, so your expenses as a shareholder would be lower, and these funds are often designed with **cost-sensitive** investors in mind.

- The positives of index funds are that they require little financial knowledge, are low cost, and are convenient to invest in. On the negative side, you could end up stuck with poorly performing assets and the potential for returns to be less than those of successful managers of actively managed funds.

- The goal of index fund managers are to mirror the performance of a particular index – and not try to outperform it, which is the goal of managers of active funds.
- Although many think that index funds are relatively new, the first publicly available index fund was launched back in the mid-1970s.
- Index funds **often perform better than actively managed funds over longer** investment time frames. Even so, there are still risks involved with this style of investing. If the tracked index falls, then your investment's value will follow and if it is at the time of your retirement or planned withdrawal, you will suffer financially, and your living conditions could be affected.
- You can reduce risk by diversifying your portfolio by holding several different index funds covering a variety of stock markets or sectors.
- Index funds can provide a very straightforward, cost-effective, and diversified way for you to steadily increase your wealth over time. Fund managers do not decide which individual investments they should buy or sell, which is what happens in active mutual funds.
- *Investors in these products expect their chosen index to rise over the long term, even if it encounters some turbulence along the way! The performance of the FTSE All-World Index, which has delivered an average annual return of 9.3% since 1993, according to Vanguard, provides a real world blueprint (30 plus years of results) of what* index funds *can achieve* **IF** *utilized appropriately.*
- So, should you choose as a novice investor an active mutual fund(s) or index fund(s)? You can spread your risk by investing a portion in each at the level that you are comfortable with. Again, index funds replicate the performance of an index, whereas the managers of mutual funds will pick and choose securities they believe will help them outperform that index. If an active manager makes the right calls, then they can substantially outperform their benchmark index and deliver handsome returns.

Popular index funds that you may want to consider include the following:

*Fidelity 500 Index Fund (FXAIX)

*Schwab S & P 500 Index Fund (SWPPX)

*T. Rowe Price Equity Index 500 Fund (PREIX)

*Vanguard 500 Index Fund Investor Shares (VFINX)

*Many others

Be sure to do your own independent research, confirm that fees are low, and you can do so by going directly to the sites by "typing in the ticker symbol" using your favorite search engine!

Target Date Funds (TDFs)

Although technically a mutual fund, **target date funds** are separated out in this bonus section in order to give you more clarity on how you can use them to build wealth.

Target-date funds are a "set it and forget it" or "invest it and rest" retirement savings option that removes two headaches for you as an investor:

1) deciding on a mix of assets which saves you time and

2) re-balancing your investments for you over time which saves you time

Target-date funds, also known as **life-cycle funds** or **target-retirement funds**—aim to continually strike the right balance between the risk necessary to build wealth and safer options to protect a growing nest egg.

The fund automatically re-balances your portfolio with the right mix of stocks, bonds and money market accounts as you age and is a great hands-off way for you to build wealth if that fits your personality and risk profile!

Target Date Funds are "mutual funds" that **purchase from other mutual funds** (known in the "investment world" as a "fund of funds") and they are designed to build a diverse portfolio. While you set and forget or invest and rest so to speak, the fund updates your asset allocation over the years for you.

Early in your working life, a target-date fund generally is set for growth by having a much larger slice of your portfolio in stocks rather than fixed-income investments like bonds, which are safer but provide smaller returns (the approach is similar to that of a 529 education savings plan). As your retirement year approaches, the fund gradually shifts toward more bonds, money market accounts and other lower-risk investments.

Your retirement year is the "target date" of most of these funds—unless you choose a target date for other purposes, and the funds are conveniently named to correspond with your planned retirement year. Say you are 35 years old and plan to work until you are 65, a Target Date 2055 would possibly be of appeal to you. Most target-date funds are named in **five-year increments with some at 10-year increments,** so you would choose the provider with a fund named with the year nearest your planned retirement date or other target date based on your goals.

Below you will find some of the more popular target date funds that you may want to consider:

Vanguard Target 2045 Fund Investor Shares VTIVX

Fidelity Freedom Index 2045 Fund Investor Class FIOFX

Lifecycle Index 2045 Fund Premier Class TLMPX

American Funds 2045 Target Date Retirement Fund Class R-5 REHTX

T Rowe Price Retirement 2045 Fund TRRKX

There are many other target date funds, and the current data is current as of market close on February 1, 2024. Be sure to do your own independent research as the accuracy of the data cannot be guaranteed.

Always realize that the main appeal of target-date funds for most is their simplicity. And just as an index fund operates with simplicity, so too does a

target date fund! The funds go from a "high ratio" of riskier equity funds to safer investments like bonds, and money market accounts as they get closer to the "target date", **freezing your asset allocation** to protect your nest egg.

An important question to ask yourself or your advisor when choosing among target-date funds is whether the account will freeze the year you plan to retire, or whether a "through" fund that continues the glide path for 5, 10, 15, or 20 years past retirement before freezing your asset allocation will be in effect. You want to plan your approach appropriately and select the fund that's right for your retirement or other goals.

How to purchase:

*through your retirement plan

*directly from fund

*open brokerage account ($500 to $3,000 to open)

Exchange Traded Funds (ETFs)

They are similar to **Mutual Funds** as just a few key differences set them apart. The biggest similarity between **ETFs** (**E**xchange-**T**raded **F**und**s**) and mutual funds are that they both represent professionally managed collections **(or "baskets")** of individual stocks, bonds or other investments.

However, investment minimums are normally lower with an ETF! You can purchase an ETF share of **Vanguard FTSE Emerging Markets** *for under $100. Many more ETF shares start at $500 or more, and you can learn more about ETF offerings by visiting VettaFi financial website.*

- It is key that you understand that **ETFs** allow you to trade **"throughout the trading day"** at market prices. This flexibility **is a key difference** in how the **fund** works as compared to a mutual fund. This level of flexibility may be utilized by active traders making moves throughout the day.

- The main difference between ETFs and mutual funds are that an ETFs price is based on the market price and is sold only in **"full"** shares. Mutual funds, however, are sold based on dollars, so **"you can specify any dollar amount"** that you'd like to invest.

- As an investor, **you have options** and can reap the benefits of diversification.

CALCULATORS Visit: TheWealthIncreaser.com

When you are investing you must know that your goals, risk-tolerance, income and your personal situation must also be taken into serious consideration.

If you currently owe $100,000 on your home mortgage and you desire to pay it off in 5 years, you will need to do some analysis and not just choose the first thing that comes to your mind. If your monthly payment is $1,000 and $500 of your mortgage payment is going toward principal, in 5 years your balance would be roughly $70,000 if you continued on that path.

By adding $1,200 to the monthly payment of $1,000 you could pay $2,200 monthly ($1,700 going toward your principal) and have your mortgage paid off in 5 years, however you would be responsible for paying your property taxes (mandatory) and insurance (optional after your home is paid off, but generally makes sense to have).

Or you could choose an investment strategy of investing the $1,200 per month for 5 years in the market and based on historical trends you could have over $90,000 after 5 years, and since you continued your mortgage payments at $500 per month in principal payments, you would owe $70,000 and therefore have an addition $20,000 plus after the payoff of your mortgage, in your pocket by doing so--assuming your returns were as expected.

In this example inflation is assumed to be 3% and your rate of return is assumed to be 9%. Even if you only assumed a rate of return of 3% (same as inflation) you would have over $80,000, which would still put you ahead by over $10,000 after the payoff of your mortgage. As long as you have a positive return you will come out ahead based on the assumptions mentioned above.

If after 5 years of investing you had a negative return you would possibly fall short of the $70,000 that was needed and you could decide to ride the market longer and pay off the mortgage later, cash in, in spite of the losses and payoff as much as you could on the mortgage.

As you can see from this example, your goals, risk tolerance, income and personal situation will play a large part in **how you decide to pay off your debt** *and how you select your investments!*

You want to know how to invest properly on the front end and you want to know that you can **invest inside of your retirement account(s)** (your earnings will grow tax free) and avoid taxes for years or **outside of your retirement account(s)** (you will provide 1099 and other paperwork to your tax professional that your brokerage would send to you at tax time) where you would possibly owe taxes on an annual basis (ETFs and Index funds are often tax efficient even outside of retirement accounts).

If you are age 25 and desire to **retire by age 55** with your house paid off and **over 4 million** in your account in today's dollars, you would have to invest $1,600 monthly for 30 years assuming 3% inflation and a 10% rate of return—and also assuming you pay your house off within that 30-year period.

Therefore, in the above examples, your returns would be affected depending on the type of investment and whether the investment is inside or outside of your retirement accounts. Once you reach age 59 1/2 you can withdraw your retirement funds without incurring an early withdrawal penalty, however you would pay taxes at your ordinary income rate, unless the distributions were from a ROTH IRA or there was an exception that applied.

Mandatory withdrawals from your traditional IRA or retirement plan would be required once you reached age 73, however with a ROTH IRA, there are no mandatory withdrawals, however after your death your beneficiaries must take required minimum distributions!

Also realize that you can choose **balanced funds** that invest in a hybrid of asset classes, whether stocks, bonds, money market instruments, or alternative investments. The objective of this fund, known as an asset allocation fund, is to reduce the risk of exposure across asset classes.

In closing, it is important that you realize that this discussion is not about theory or what you possibly need to do, but what you **CAN** do! You must at this time analyze your income and expenses and determine your discretionary income that you have available so that you can start investing now, get more income by creating a plan to increase your income whether by the payoff of your debt, scaling back on your entertainment and other expenses, or finding other ways to get income on a consistent basis.

Although you will hear many financial planners tout the fact that you can increase your savings and come up with a significant amount to invest by scaling back on the $5 that you spend daily on your favorite latte or coffee, that is not something that we are a big proponent of as we realize that for some, a $5 cup of coffee can give them the added energy that is needed to help them earn more on a daily, weekly and annual basis, therefore they more than offset the $100 or so that they spend on a monthly basis on coffee that they could be using for investing.

However there are other ways that you can get more income and cut expenses and you may want to analyze and pursue them!

Once you determine the amount of income that you have available to invest and you commit to investing that or another amount over a "period of time" **you can start on a path to reaching the number that you need to attain your goal(s)** and live daily with more joy on the inside!

Whether your discretionary or available funds to invest are $200 per month or $2,000 per month and you decide to use it to invest long-term, you can achieve significant results over a 30-year period. By calculating what you can do now, **(you need to know your discretionary or available income that you have to invest, whether you will invest weekly, monthly, yearly or a one-time lump-sum investment and furthermore you need to know the "time frame that is needed or desired" to reach your goal)** you can determine the nest egg that you can have by investing consistently in a relatively painless way—starting today.

Investing $200 monthly at 3% inflation and a 9% rate of return will give you over $500,000 (five-hundred thousand) in 30 years!

The 4 percent raise that you get, the promotion that you get, or working one or two days a month for lyft, uber, grubhub or other "new economy" options can easily provide you that cushion to invest either temporarily or permanently over the next 30 years.

In many cases, you can find $200 by analyzing your monthly spending and tightening up your budget some. You can do a detailed analysis of your insurance products, taxes and other areas of your finances and discover new savings or increases in income. The ways that you can come up with the needed funds for long-term wealth building success is endless, if you want to achieve your goals in a sincere manner!

Investing $2,000 monthly at 3% inflation and a 9% rate of return will give you over $5,000,000 (five million) in 30 years!

To get that extra $2,000 per month, you may have to start a business, have your stay-at-home spouse find employment either part-time or full-time, or determine other ways to increase your monthly income based on your creativity and the unique skills that you now have or will cultivate in the near future.

In many instances high net worth and high-income earners wasted hundreds if not thousands on a monthly basis on frivolous or unnecessary spending that could be utilized more appropriately for building long-term wealth of significant amounts.

What is the **discretionary amount** that you "need or want to get to" so that you can invest at this time and in your future, to work towards making life more manageable for you and your loved ones?

How You Can Invest using Mutual Funds, Index Funds, Target Date Funds and Exchange-Traded-Funds:

1. Make sure you have a brokerage account with enough cash on hand, and with access to mutual fund shares and other investments.
2. Identify specific mutual funds or ETFs that match your investing goals in terms of risk, returns, fees, and minimum investments. Some brokerage platforms offer fund screening and research tools.

3. Determine how much you want to invest initially and submit your trade. If you choose, you can set up automatic recurring investments in the amount that you desire.
4. Monitor and review performances periodically, making adjustments as needed.
5. When it is time to close your position, enter a sell order on your platform.
6. Realize that with some funds you can invest directly and depending on the fund type, the functions mentioned above will be done by the fund manager or brokerage.

While many mutual funds are no-load, you can often avoid brokerage fees and commissions by purchasing a fund directly from the mutual fund company instead of going through an intermediary or third party.

There are pros and cons of investing utilizing mutual funds and you can go to investopedia.com to learn more about investing in a simplified, yet effective manner!

Some funds are defined with a specific allocation strategy that is fixed, so the investor can have a predictable exposure to various asset classes. Other funds follow a strategy for dynamic allocation percentages to meet various investor objectives. This may include responding to market conditions, business cycle changes, or the changing phases of the investor's own life.

The portfolio manager is commonly given the freedom to switch the ratio of asset classes as needed to maintain the integrity of the fund's stated strategy.

Below you will find what is often included in mutual funds, including balanced funds, index funds, target date funds, and exchange-traded funds.

Money Market Funds

The money market consists of safe, risk-free, short-term debt instruments, mostly government Treasury bills. An investor will not earn substantial returns, but the principal is guaranteed. A typical return is a little more than the amount earned in a regular checking or savings account and a little less than the average certificate of deposit (CD).

Income Funds

Income funds are named for their purpose: to provide current income on a steady basis. These funds invest primarily in government and high-quality corporate debt, holding these bonds until maturity to provide interest streams. While fund holdings may appreciate, the primary objective of these funds are to provide steady cash flow to investors. As such, the audience for these funds consists of conservative investors and retirees.

International/Global Funds

An international fund, or foreign fund, invests only in assets located outside an investor's home country. Global funds, however, can invest anywhere around the world. Their volatility often depends on the unique country's economy and political risks. However, these funds can be part of a well-balanced portfolio by increasing diversification, since the returns in foreign countries may be uncorrelated with returns at home.

Specialty Funds

Sector funds are targeted strategy funds aimed at specific sectors of the economy, such as financial, technology, or health care. Sector funds can be extremely volatile since the stocks in a given sector tend to be highly correlated with each other.

Regional funds make it easier to focus on a specific geographic area of the world. This can mean focusing on a broader region or an individual country.

Socially responsible funds, or ethical funds, invest only in companies that meet the criteria of certain guidelines or beliefs. For example, some socially responsible funds do not invest in "sin" industries such as tobacco, alcoholic beverages, weapons, or nuclear power. Other funds invest primarily in green technology, such as solar and wind power or recycling. Fidelity Charitable and other "Socially Responsible Investment Funds" are now available in abundance in the investment world.

Other

Bond, precious metals, natural resources, crypto and other investment products are now packaged and sold as mutual funds in some instances.

You can **use the above approaches** to ensure you reach your "retirement number" or "other goals" that you have—and use other riskier or more aggressive approaches to further build wealth if you are in position to do so.

Investing a **percentage of** your investments in mutual funds, index funds, target date funds and ETF funds can be a painless and simple way for you to build wealth and live out your retirement with dignity. Automatic Investing (dollar-cost averaging) $200 monthly in a mutual fund, $200 monthly in an index fund, $200 monthly in a target date fund and $200 monthly in an ETF fund **(total of $800 monthly)** will provide you with a hefty return over time, if market trends continue. You can also invest $200 per week and invest automatically if you feel that will work better for you.

The above approaches, along with your social security, pension, and possibly other retirement income can put you well ahead of most, if you start early and invest consistently. You no longer must fake it until you make it, you can now be true to yourself as you are now on a serious path toward making your dreams come true, because you decided to take your mind off the shelf!

Isn't it time that you use a "more pragmatic approach" toward investing and building wealth?

Always realize that you have **numerous options** to choose from in the investment world regardless of your goals, however the process of **investing in an effective manner is not that complicated,** unless you make it complicated. In this short (relative to what you have learned) **bonus section**, you have learned how you can invest in a straightforward manner and achieve realistic results that can enhance your living conditions while you are here on planet earth.

All the best to your tax, investment, and wealth building success...

Publisher: TFA Financial Planning

Email: tj@TheWealthIncreaser.com

Thomas (TJ) Underwood is the CEO of TFA Financial Planning—one of the most successful tax and financial planning companies in the Atlanta metropolitan area. TFA Financial Planning is based out of Atlanta, Georgia.

Thomas (TJ) Underwood is a former fee-only financial planner and top producing loan processor, and he has assisted clients from as far away as Germany with their financial concerns. The concepts in "The Art of Essential Action" have been utilized by savvy individuals to help them build wealth and achieve many of their major wealth building goals.

The concepts, strategies and approaches to wealth building in this guide are designed to enhance successful outcomes for those who desire to utilize proven systems and maximum effort to achieve meaningful goals during the various stages of their life cycle.

Thomas (TJ) Underwood is also the creator of TheWealthIncreaser.com, one of the leading financial blog sites that can be found in the internet universe.

The Art of Essential Action

A Financial Guide for Taking Essential Action and Using Time Management More Wisely so that You Can Achieve More

ISBN: 978-1-953994-27-1

Publisher: TFA Financial Planning

Email: tj@TheWealthIncreaser.com

Made in the USA
Monee, IL
04 November 2026

67387305R10125